Contemporary Italy

Contemporary Italy

A Research Guide

Martin J. Bull

Bibliographies and Indexes in World History,
Number 43

Greenwood Press
Westport, Connecticut • London

Library of Congress Cataloging-in-Publication Data

Bull, Martin J.
    Contemporary Italy : a research guide / Martin J. Bull.
        p.   cm.—(Bibliographies and indexes in world history, ISSN
    0742–6852 ; no. 43)
    Includes bibliographical references and index.
    ISBN 0–313–29137–3 (alk. paper)
    1. Italy—Politics and government—1945– —Bibliography.
    2. Italy—Economic conditions—1945– —Bibliography. 3. Italy—
    Social conditions—1945– —Bibliography. I. Title. II. Series.
    Z2360.3.B85 1996
    [DG577]
    016.945092—dc20   95–39488

British Library Cataloguing in Publication Data is available.

Library of Congress Catalog Card Number: 95–39488
ISBN: 0–313–29137–3
ISSN: 0742–6852

First published in 1996

Greenwood Press, 88 Post Road West, Westport, CT 06881
An imprint of Greenwood Publishing Group, Inc.

Printed in the United States of America

The paper used in this book complies with the
Permanent Paper Standard issued by the National
Information Standards Organization (Z39.48–1984).

10 9 8 7 6 5 4 3 2

Copyright Acknowledgment

Excerpts from "Italy" by Martin J. Bull in *Southern European Studies Guide,* edited by Dr. John
Loughlin, were reprinted with kind permission of Bowker-Saur, a division of Reed Elsevier (UK)
Ltd.

To Maria
for her tolerance and support

Contents

viii   Contents

List of Abbreviations

AA.VV	Autori varie (Various Authors).
ACLI	*Associazione cristiana dei lavoratori italiani* (Christian Association of Italian Workers).
AN	*Alleanza nazionale* (National Alliance).
ASMI	Association for the Study of Modern Italy.
CENSIS	*Centro studi investimenti sociali* (Centre for Social Investment Studies).
CGIL	*Confederazione generale italiana del lavoro* (Italian General Confederation of Labour).
CERES	*Centro di studi socioeconomici* (Centre of Socio-Economic Studies).
CIA	Central Intelligence Agency.
COBAS	*Comitati di base* (Grassroots Committees).
CONGRIPS	Conference Group on Italian Politics and Society.
CUB	*Comitati unitari di base* (Grassroots Unitary Committees).
DC	*Democrazia Cristiana* (Christian Democracy).
DP	*Democrazia proletaria* (Proletarian Democracy).
EC	European Community.
EEC	European Economic Community.
EIU	Economist Intelligence Unit.
ENI	*Ente nazionale idrocarburi* (National Agency of Hydrocarbons).
EU	European Union.
Eurispes	*Istituto di studi politici, economici e sociali* (Institute of Political, Economic and Social Studies).
IRI	*Istituto per la ricostruzione industriale* (Institute for Industrial Reconstruction).
ISAP	*Istituto per la scienza dell'amministrazione pubblica* (Institute for the Science of Public Administration).
ISTAT	*Istituto centrale di statistica* (Central Institute of Statistics).
MSI	*Movimento sociale italiano* (Italian Social Movement).
MSI-DN	*Movimento sociale italiano — Destra nazionale* (Italian Social Movement - National Right).
NATO	North Atlantic Treaty Organisation.
OECD	Organisation for Economic Cooperation and Development.
P2	*Propaganda due* (Propaganda Two).
PCI	*Partito comunista italiano* (Italian Communist Party).
PDS	*Partito democratico della sinistra* (Democratic Party of the Left).
PDUP	*Partito di unità proletaria per il comunismo* (Democratic Party of Proletarian Unity for Communism).

PLI   *Partito liberale italiano* (Italian Liberal Party).
PR   *Partito radicale* (Radical Party).
PRI   *Partito repubblicano italiano* (Italian Republican Party).
PSDI   *Partito socialista democratico italiano* (Italian Social Democratic Party).
PSI   *Partito socialista italiano* (Italian Socialist Party).
PSIUP   *Partito socialista italiano d'unità proletaria* (Italian Socialist Party of Proletarian Unity).
RC   *Rifondazione comunista* (Reconstructed Communism).
SISP   *Società Italiana di Scienza Politica* (Italian Political Science Association).

Using the Research Guide

The introduction outlines the context within which the evolution of Italian contemporary studies should be viewed. The book is subsequently divided into two parts. The first part is a survey and analysis which is divided, by subject area, into five chapters: history, politics, government, economy and society. The chapters themselves are divided analytically into sections and (where necessary) sub-sections. The second part of the book is an annotated bibliographic guide to the works referred to in the first part. Its structure, therefore, follows that of Part One: it is divided into five chapters and the same sections and sub-sections. Since each work is annotated, it means that Part Two of the book constitutes a guide in itself which can be used independently of the main text. Each work has a numerical reference. In Part One this number appears in square parentheses after the date of publication of the work being discussed. In Part Two, the number appears before the citation in the left margin. Each numerical reference is decimalised, e.g. 1.51, 2.34, 3.67, 4.101, 5.133. The first part of the number indicates the chapter of the bibliography in which the work appears. The second part of the number indicates exactly where it is to be found in that chapter in the bibliography. For example, a work numbered [2.34] in Part One indicates that this is the thirty-fourth work appearing in Chapter 2 of Part Two. The numerical referencing across the chapters is not cumulative in that each chapter in the bibliography starts afresh from one (i.e. 1.1, 2.1, 3.1, 4.1, 5.1). A subject index and separate author index complete the book. The indexes are keyed to page numbers, not entry numbers.

Preface

This is a historiographic and annotated bibliographic guide to the study of contemporary Italy. It includes over six hundred texts in history, politics, government, the economy and society which have characterised and shaped the academic and scholarly study of contemporary Italy. The book is intended primarily as a guide for English, North American and Italian scholars who have either just begun their studies on Italy or who are specialists in specific areas of Italian studies but who would benefit from knowledge of what has been published in subject areas with which they may not be familiar. The texts have been selected with certain criteria in mind.

Firstly, an attempt has been made to provide a genuine mix between works in English and Italian. Where, on a few occasions, it has proved necessary to choose between works of equal quality and importance, those written or available in English have been given priority. However, a glance through the bibliography will confirm that this has not affected the high percentage of Italian works cited, and that a genuine mix of materials has been achieved.

Secondly, emphasis has been given to recent literature, i.e. works published in the last ten to fifteen years, and which are still in print. This is not only because these works are most obviously available but also because (as the Introduction points out), it is the last twenty years which have seen the most significant changes in Italian society and advances in Italian studies. This criterion, however, has not been applied rigidly. Where there is an absence of recent material or where older texts represent important contributions to the development of Italian studies, the older material has been cited.

Thirdly, the works are those which have appeared in monograph form, whether single-authored, joint-authored or edited. This includes yearbooks, data books, surveys and various sources of information (statistical and other). There are few exceptions to the monograph rule. Where there have been substantial chapters in a book which have filled an important gap in the absence of a monograph, these works have been cited, and where, in the case of the economy, journals provide regular reports, these too have been cited. But these are exceptions to the rule.

Fourthly, the works chosen focus on 'contemporary' Italy. By this is meant primarily postwar Italy, but the key histories which are essential to understanding Italy since Unification have also been included.

There has been no rigid number of texts adhered to for each subject area. The difference in the number of texts cited between chapters (which, in a book of this scope, could be said to be marginal) is not a reflection of the perceived importance of the subject matters, but rather of the amount of good material which has been published in each area. However, for reasons of space, some subject areas have either been excluded or received much less attention than they would otherwise merit. Anthropology and culture have not been tackled in any depth, although several general works on culture have been included in Chapter 5 on society. Political and social theory have been excluded, and urban studies remains largely undeveloped.

The potential minefield of 'forthcomings' has been avoided by excluding works which are not yet published unless I have received evidence that the book is to be published shortly and have gained some knowledge of the contents of the manuscript. If everything 'forthcoming' were to be included, it would expose a book of this sort to many factual errors, given the tendency of publishers to advertise titles of books which have not yet been completed.

A work of this scope could not have been completed successfully without the assistance of others, and I am indebted to a number of people and institutions. Inspiration for this book came from a short bibliographic essay (entitled 'Italy') I wrote in John Loughlin (ed), *Southern European Studies Guide* (London: Bowker-Saur, 1993). Even though the current book bears little structural relation to that essay, there is nevertheless a similarity in the kernel of texts identified in the two pieces of work, some annotations of these texts remains the same, and the current book's introduction is a significantly expanded version of the two paragraphs which introduce the earlier essay. Some of the annotations and parts of the text, therefore, are reprinted with kind permission of Bowker-Saur, a division of Reed Elsevier (UK) Ltd.

Part of the research was carried out in my capacity as a Visiting Fellow in the Department of Political and Social Sciences at the European University Insitute, Florence, during 1992-93, and I should like to thank the EUI for the provision of facilities and services during my stay there. At the University of Salford I should like to acknowledge the financial support of the Department of Politics and Contemporary History, the European Studies Research Institute and the University Research Fund, which allowed me to carry out two essential field trips to Italy, one at the beginning of the research and the other (as a follow-up) once the bulk of the writing had been completed. Martin Alexander, Mike Goldsmith and Geoff Harris were unfailing in their support for this project and did everything they could to assist in its speedy completion.

A number of people have commented on the text or parts of it. Paul Ginsborg brought his wealth of expertise to bear on a preliminary draft of the book and made a number of invaluable comments and suggestions. Luciano Bardi, Maurizio Cotta, Stephen Hellman, Peter Lange, James Newell, Serge Noiret, and Martin Rhodes read and commented on my earlier essay, and I was able to use their suggestions to help design the structure and content of this book. Alice Kelikian and Perry Willson offered useful comments on specific parts of the text.

For their bibliographic assistance I should like to thank Tony Curran, Peter Kennealy, Serge Noiret, the European University Institute's library, the *Biblioteca Nazionale* in Florence, the *Istituto Gramsci* in Rome and the University of Salford library. I should also like to thank various publishers for their co-operation in forwarding me back lists, current catalogues and inspection copies. For secretarial support I am indebted to Kath Capper, Mary Cenci and Heather Lally. Finally, I should like to thank the Senior Editors for Reference Books at Greenwood Press, Mildred Vasan and Cynthia Harris, for their patience and professional assistance in the production of the book. Responsibility for the final selection of, and comments on, the texts remains mine alone.

This is, ultimately, a selective and not a comprehensive guide. Any selection can be viewed as arbitrary, but readers must be left to judge for themselves the value of mine against the aims of the book and the criteria governing the selection noted above. Inevitably, some authors may feel aggrieved at what they may feel is the unjustifiable exclusion of certain works from the guide. At times, decisions as to whether or not to include a text were made with difficulty. It is to be hoped that aggrieved authors will not hesitate to write to me, if only for the fact that the exclusion of their work may be due to oversight and not deliberate choice, something which is an obvious danger in an extended work of this sort. Certainly, any suggestions from readers of this book will be most welcome in order that it may be improved for any future edition.

Martin Bull,
Salford, July 1995

Introduction

THE EVOLUTION OF RESEARCH ON CONTEMPORARY ITALY

First lines are often revealing about prevailing attitudes towards a country:

Italy is universally considered a particularly unpredictable and deceptive country.[1]

The Italian political system is like no other Western democracy.[2]

Italy invites hyperbole. Almost everything about it appears monumental.[3]

These examples are selected at random from a personal library, but they reflect the conventional wisdom about Italy: that it is an unusual and fascinating country which fails to fit the usual patterns of historical, social, economic and political development which characterise other advanced western democracies. For a long time, however, the academic study of Italy failed to rise to the challenge of this fascination and apparent uniqueness. Indeed, the quality and quantity of scholarship published on Italian contemporary history, politics, the economy and society (particularly in English-language materials) has improved substantially only in the period since the 1970s. Until then there was a shortage both of Anglo-American specialists on Italy ('Italianists'), and of key native works available for, and worthy of, translation.[4] This shortage was a product both of the lateness in the development of the respective disciplines in Italy and of the differences between the Italian and Anglo-Saxon academic traditions, differences particularly noteworthy in the disciplines of history, sociology and political science.

In the social sciences and humanities in Italy the line between professional scholarship and personal and political engagement has always been a tenuous one. Italian historians, for example, have been to a large extent divided into schools of thought which reflect the fundamental divisions persisting in Italian society. History writing, therefore, has to a large extent been what Martin Clark has described as 'committed' history, 'designed to cheer on their own team', whether the team be liberals, catholics, radicals or marxists. This has been reinforced by the influence of Croce, standard reading for most Italian postwar historians, whose style laid emphasis on ideas and men rather than on structures; and by the influence of the Italian communist and socialist parties over history writing, (primarily, but not solely, through their control over journals and reviews) with their obvious emphasis on ideology, social protest and class struggle. Obviously, these influences can still produce good history, but much of it is selective and either apologetic or critical. Overall comprehensiveness has suffered as a result. Besides lacunae in the treatment of social and economic history, what has perhaps been most neglected is the history of government, institutions and the state, something which historians have only really taken up in earnest since the mid-1980s.

Sociology and political science obtained academic legitimacy much later than history and their full professionalisation dates only from the 1970s. The Marxist-Crocean influence (referred to above) bred a resistance to empirical research which was not overcome until after the mid-1960s (see below). Sociologists in the 1950s and 1960s were essentially products of the 'modernisation' model of growth which Italy appeared to be undergoing, and sociology tended to be confined to social and economic research centres usually linked to regional planning agencies. In the 1970s many of the self-same sociologists, reacting, in a changed climate, to the optimistic assumptions of the previous decades, became associated with the political activism on the left, and sociology became associated with trade union study centres which focused on subjects such as interest groups and the industrial working class. There is no denying the quality of some of this work, which resulted in sociology's full professionalisation, and the assistance it provided in housing political scientists in their search for autonomy (which has left these two disciplines intimately related). The number of sociologists, however, has remained small.

Political science, paradoxically (in view of the fact that the discipline is commonly regarded as having been born in Italy), has been the slowest of the social sciences to mature. Indeed, it is the failure of this discipline to consolidate itself in the postwar period which has been the Achilles' heel of contemporary Italian studies. As late as 1973, when Percy Allum produced what was for a long time the standard English text on Italian politics and government, *Italy — Republic Without Government?* [2.4] the author referred to 'an up and coming school of political science.' The vast quantity of literature on Italian government and politics, he noted, consisted of either treatises on constitutional and public law or polemical journalism. The explanation for this vacuum was essentially political: the discipline's association with Fascism. Social science faculties were instituted in 1924 and it became quickly apparent that their essential function was to train cadres for the new regime. This association with Fascism placed the discipline under suspicion in the postwar period, and, coupled with skepticism from catholics and Croce-inspired historians (about the utility and value of an 'empirical science') and even from Marxists (about an American 'bourgeois science' insensitive to analysis of class struggle) ensured that the discipline was slow in developing its own autonomy.

Consequently, classic Italian political science texts from the turn of the century by authors such as Michels, Mosca and Pareto were widely read abroad but were relatively unknown in postwar Italy, obscured as they were by the preponderance of legal and constitutional-inspired texts. The 'rebirth' (as it effectively was) of Italian political science was a product of a combination of factors. Two of the principal ones were the efforts of individuals such as Norberto Bobbio and Giovanni Sartori, and the 'Americanization' of the discipline (through the funding of empirical studies by American foundations and the training of a generation of Italian academics in the United States). Subsequently, the 1970s saw the expansion of the discipline with its own journal (the *Rivista Italiana di Scienza Politica*, with others following) and professional body (the *Società Italiana di Scienza Politica*, SISP).

The common turning point, however, for both political science and sociology came with a series of studies financed by the Twentieth Century Fund and carried out by a team of researchers outside the formal university structure at the Carlo Cattaneo Institute in Bologna in the mid-1960s. The four volume study (later expanded to six), which was subsequently synthesised by Giorgio Galli and Alfonso Prandi into one volume for English readers (*Patterns of Political Participation in Italy* (1970) [2.28]), gave an enormous boost to empirical research in Italy and remains one of the most in-depth analyses available of the two most important political parties, the Christian Democrats (DC) and the Communists (PCI).

A common factor behind the expansion of the disciplines (which also explains the growing interest of foreign scholars) has been fascination with Italy's dualistic and (relative to other European countries) apparently anomalous development. Once the optimistic assumptions of modernisation theory were shattered by the Italian crisis of the 1970s, the peculiarities and development of the Italian model of democracy (and thus the difficulty of identifying Italy as either 'southern' or 'northern' European), and its implications for social science theories of development, acted as a magnet of attraction for many scholars.

The presence and (until the late 1970s) growing strength of the largest communist party in the west constituted the primary factor in this attraction in as far as it accounted for the failure of the political system to achieve genuine alternation in government. Two key books symbolise this early interest. Giorgio Galli, *Il bipartitismo imperfetto. Comunisti e democristiani in Italia* (1984) [2.29] identified Italy's problems as being the result of the failure to achieve alternation in government, itself a product of the strength of the two sub-cultures, catholic and Marxist. Giovanni Sartori responded with his own model of 'polarised pluralism' (best portrayed in *Parties and Party Systems: A Framework for Analysis* (1976) [2.37] and, in a collection of his writings on parties, *Teoria dei partiti e caso italiano* (1982) [2.38]). Sartori emphasised the degree of polarisation in the Italian party system. The presence of strong anti-system parties at both ends of the political spectrum effectively compelled the main party of the centre (the DC) to govern indefinitely to keep the extremes out, and the political system's problems flowed from this dilemma. The similarities and differences between the two models is not at issue here. What is important to note is that the prominence of the models as explanations of Italy's apparent instability resulted in the debate on parties and the sub-cultures becoming the focus of contemporary Italian political studies. Arguably, this focus was too narrow to be helpful to the broadening of sociology and political science (as will be noted below). On the other hand, the quality of Angelo Panebianco's recent *Political Parties: Organisation and Power* (1988) [2.33] (recognised as one of the best theoretical and comparative works on political parties for many years) is perhaps testimony to the effect of Italian political science's focus on the study of political parties.

The movement of good historians onto the 'contemporary' terrain (i.e. post-1950s), and the pursuit of new directions of research, has also considerably improved the quality of literature available, as the work of Paul Ginsborg [1.7], Silvio Lanaro [1.10] Pietro Scoppola [1.17] and Aurelio Lepre [1.11] testifies. Furthermore, publication of good material has been possible through the development of scholarly Italian journals. Outside Italy, both Britain and the United States have developed associations (the *Association for the Study of Modern Italy*, ASMI, and the *Conference Group on Italian Politics and Society*, CONGRIPS) which act as a focal point for Italianists, and journals devoted specifically to the study of Italy are, in the mid-1990s, a new and welcome phenomenon.

This is not to suggest, however, that any level of comprehensiveness has been achieved in contemporary Italian studies. On the contrary, the 'late start' of Italian social sciences and the way they subsequently developed have left considerable imbalances in the subject matters studied, as this book suggests. The most glaring imbalances are in the study of politics and government. The dominance of political parties in Italy (referred to as *partitocrazia*, literally 'rule by parties') coupled with the prolonged effect of the Galli-Sartori debate, has resulted in a predominance of studies on parties (and within that area, a predominance of studies on the PCI) to the neglect of other important subject areas. Over a forty year period, for example, almost half of foreign studies and one-fifth of Italian-based studies have been on political parties. This does not mean that all other areas have been neglected. Elections and electoral behaviour, sub-national government, the welfare state, and political attitudes and values have, for example, constituted important areas of research. Some areas have also demonstrated the capacity (as the study of parties has) to produce general texts of a seminal nature. The new wave of political science research on regional governments from 1970 onwards, for example, produced, twelve years later, one of the most sophisticated explanations of institutional performance available today, linking, as it does, institutional performance to questions of culture: Robert Putnam, with Robert Leonardi and Raffaella Nanetti, *Making Democracy Work. Civic Tradition in Italy* (1992) [2.20]. Nevertheless, not enough scholarly research has been conducted in a wide range of areas including government institutions, public policy and political economy and foreign policy and international relations. The fact that Italy is currently under the international spotlight because of the crisis it is enduring should not be misinterpreted as an unequivocal sign that past limitations will now be overcome. While there are signs that this crisis is reinvigorating (and modifying) scholarly agendas for research, these should not be confused with a wealth of literature which is inspired more by ephemeral journalistic and publishing opportunities than academic research.

Finally, as will become apparent from the number of Italian texts listed in this book, even when good work appears in Italian, not enough of it is published in English, despite the considerable amount of foreign literature published in Italian each year. This problem is ultimately reflected in the failure of Italy to gain the status and prominence in comparative scholarship experienced by countries such as France and Germany. Italian scholars, on the one hand, study mainly Italy with little attention to other countries. Foreign comparative scholars without a good command of Italian, on the other hand, are too often confronted with negligible published sources. Things are changing, but it remains true that the study of Italy remains primarily the preserve of Italian specialists. Comparativists too often overlook Italy, either when studying the 'big four' western nations (Britain, the United States, France and Germany) or when analysing the Mediterranean belt (Spain, Portugal, and Greece). Overcoming this limitation is crucial to the country's emergence as a true international field of study.

NOTES

1.   Luigi Barzini, *The Europeans* (Harmondsworth: Penguin, 1983), p.157, first line of chapter 5, entitled 'The Flexible Italians'.

2.   Frederic Spotts and Theodor Weiser, *Italy. A Difficult Democracy* [2.22], p.1.

3.   Joseph LaPalombara, *Democracy Italian Style* [2.16], p.ix.

4.   The shortage of works in English is evident from the bibliography edited by Peter Lange in the 1970s: *Studies on Italy 1943-1975. Select Bibliography of American and British Materials in Political Science, Economics, Sociology and Anthropology* (Torino: Edizioni della fondazione srl, 1977). Many sections of the bibliography are so sparse that they made Italy at the time virtually impenetrable for the non-Italian reader.

Part One

SURVEY AND ANALYSIS

1
History

GENERAL WORKS

Giuliano Procacci, *History of the Italian People* (1991) [1.15] and Harry Hearder, *Italy. A Short History* (1990) [1.8] provide overviews of Italian history from the classical era to the modern day. The best history of Italy since Unification is Martin Clark, *Modern Italy, 1871-1982* (1984) [1.2]. While some readers might still prefer Dennis Mack Smith's *Italy: A Modern History* (1969) [1.13], Clark's has more extensive coverage of the postwar period. Useful texts for the beginner are Christopher Duggan, *A Concise History of Italy* (1994) [1.6] and Spencer M. Di Scala, *Italy. From Revolution to Republic* (1995) [1.5]. The best overall economic history is the multi-volume Valerio Castronovo, *La storia economica d'Italia* (1975) [1.1].

On postwar Italy, strictly political histories are provided by Norman Kogan, *A Political History of Post-War Italy: from the Old to the New Centre-Left* (1981) [1.9], and Giuseppe Mammarella, *Italia Contemporanea (1943-1985)* (1986) [1.14]. These histories have been surpassed in recent years by works which attempt to integrate social, economic and political history. Paul Ginsborg, *A History of Contemporary Italy. Society and Politics 1943-1988* (1990) [1.7] is exemplary of this trend and is the best history, in English, of the postwar period. Indeed, if one had to recommend a single text to English readers to prompt them into studying contemporary Italy this would be it. Ginsborg displays a masterly command over a wealth of resources and brilliantly charts Italy's postwar transformation from a largely agricultural society into an advanced industrial democracy. He identifies the social, economic and political distortions and imbalances that this transformation has entailed, and the Italian obsession with (and failure to carry through) reform. The inclusion of an excellent statistical appendix makes this text a standard reference point for all studies on contemporary Italy.

The three other most recent postwar histories are only available in Italian, but they can be usefully compared with that of Ginsborg.[1] Pietro Scoppola, *La Repubblica dei partiti: profilo storico della democrazia in Italia, 1945-1990* (1991) [1.17] is a conventional political and constitutional history (despite the introduction's claim that it is also a social history). The author's objective is to explain the historical roots and development of the malfunctioning of the Italian political system, and his focus is on the political parties. Silvio Lanaro, *Storia dell'Italia repubblicana: dalla fine della guerra agli anni novanta* (1992) [1.10] is less good as a chronological history than the other works. It tends to treat a number of different themes in historical perspective. Its particular strengths are in its treatment of the economic and social changes which Italy has undergone in the postwar period, and its analysis of cultural history (to which the other works devote little). Aurelio Lepre, *Storia della Prima Repubblica: L'Italia dal*

1942 al 1992 (1993) [1.11] is a briefer but astutely-written history of the Republic until 1992. Between them, these four texts provide a comprehensive overview of the themes of Italian postwar history and the contrasting approaches of historians in tackling them.

A useful historical aid for the beginner and a reminder of facts for the specialist is Frank Coppa (ed), *Dictionary of Modern Italian History* (1985) [1.4]. Produced by a team of American Italianists, the dictionary surveys the main events, institutions, systems and problems of Italy from the eighteenth century to the present. A useful chronological reference is provided by *Compact storia d'Italia. Cronologia 1815-1990* (1991) [1.3] which also selects certain themes for more detailed treatment for each year. For those interested in the historical analysis of certain concepts and themes (i.e. as opposed to general chronological analyses) Romano Ruggiero (ed), *Storia D'Italia: Annali* (1978-) [1.16], is a useful resource. For a general thematic overview of the work of Italian (and other) historians Fabio Levi et al. (eds), *Il Mondo Contemporaneo. Storia D'Italia* (1978) [1.12] (in three volumes), is an indispensable resource.

SECOND WORLD WAR

The most useful texts on Italy and the Second World War are F. F. Tosi et al., *L'Italia nella seconda guerra mondiale e nella resistenza* (1988) [1.25] and Simona Colarizzi, *La seconda guerra mondiale e la Repubblica* (1984) [1.20]. The most notable book in English is Richard Lamb, *War in Italy 1943-1945. A Brutal Story* (1993) [1.22] which describes the sequence of events from the fall of Mussolini until the final victory and uses previously unused archive documents in Britain, Italy and the Vatican. It is the only book in English which deals in detail with this period and is a rivetting read, although it does not take into account some interpretations of the period which have appeared in Italian, such as those of the Resistance.

Until recently there were three main texts on the Resistance: R. Battaglia, *Storia della Resistenza* (1964) [1.19], Guido Quazza, *Resistenza e Storia d'Italia* (1976) [1.24], and Charles Delzell, *Mussolini's Enemies: The Italian Anti-Fascist Resistance* (1974) [1.21]. The publication of Claudio Pavone, *Una guerra civile: saggio storico sulla moralità nella Resistenza* (1991) [1.23], however, is a landmark in the study of the Resistance and indispensable reading for anyone concerned with this period of Italian history. The product of twenty years research, it is the first book to document the history of the Resistance from the perspective of the participants themselves and consequently is the most complete analysis of the internal nature of the movement. Using the clandestine press, diaries, memoirs and party political documentation, the author reconstructs the political and psychological motivations of the participants along three analytical interpretations of the Resistance: as a patriotic war (for national independence against the Germans), a civil war (for democracy and the control of territory against the fascists) and a class war (for the achievement of an anti-capitalist social revolution). Of these, the book's most important contribution is in resurrecting (or reinforcing) the idea of the Resistance as a civil war.[2]

One further book on the period of the war which should be mentioned is Roger Absalom, *A Strange Alliance: Aspects of Escape and Survival in Italy 1943-45* (1991) [1.18]. This is the first exploration of a new archival resource discovered by the author: 85,000 files of the Allied Screening Commission consisting of applications by Italians (nearly all peasants) after the war for compensation for assistance provided to members of the Allied forces who had escaped from prison camps after 8th. September and the Armistice, these applications often being accompanied by individual reports by members of the Allied forces of their own experiences. The book provides a new insight into the nature of the peasant world during the war and its heroism.

POSTWAR SETTLEMENT

The postwar settlement has generated an entire body of literature, most of which is in Italian. Particularly noteworthy are: Massimo Legnani (ed), *L'Italia dal 1943 al 1948. Lotte politiche e sociale* (1973) [1.37]; Istituto nazionale per la storia del movimento di Liberazione in Italia, *L'Italia dalla Liberazione alla Repubblica* (1977) [1.36]; the multi-authored *Italia 1945-48. Le origini della Repubblica* (1974) [1.26]; Renzo De Felice (ed), *Resistenza e Repubblica, 1943-1956* (1985) [1.31]; and AA.VV, *La società italiana dalla Resistenza alla guerra fredda* (1989) [1.27].

Two books in English also provide some first class scholarship on this period: David Ellwood, *Italy, 1943-1945* (1985) [1.32], and Stuart Woolf (ed), *The Rebirth of Italy, 1943-1953* (1972) [1.47], which provides a thematic study of the postwar settlement by a group of specialists. Specific treatments of the economic and industrial reconstruction of Italy (and its political implications) are provided by: Mariuccia Salvati, *Stato e industria nella ricostruzione. Alle origini del potere democristiano 1944/1949* (1982) [1.43]; Carlo Daneo, *La politica economica della ricostruzione 1945-49* (1975) [1.30]; and Bruzio Manzocchi, *Lineamenti di politica economica in Italia (1945-1949)* (1960) [1.39]. The differences between the North and the South of Italy during the liberation and the reconstruction period are of fundamental importance to understanding the subsequent development of the Republic. Two studies provide an illuminating contrast in this respect: Fabio Levi, Paride Rugafiori and S. Vento, *Il triangolo industriale tra ricostruzione e lotta di classe, 1945-1948* (1974) [1.38], and Nicola Gallerano (ed), *L'altro dopoguerra. Roma e il Sud 1943-1945* (1985) [1.34].

Book length studies of the Italian Constitution and the manner in which it was drafted have failed to attract foreign scholars. There are many such studies in Italian of which the most comprehensive is the multi-volume G. Branca (ed), *Commentario della costituzione* (1975-) [1.28], which uses different authors to analyse the constitution article by article. The best single volumes are: Piero Calamandrei and P. Levi, *Commentario sistematico alla costituzione italiana* (1950) [1.29]; V. Falzone, F. Palermo and F. Consentino (eds), *La Costituzione della Repubblica italiana* (1976) [1.33]; and (more on the politics behind the drafting) Umberto Terracini (a member of the Italian Communist Party in the Constituent Assembly), *Come nacque la Costituzione* (1978) [1.45]. The full text of the Constitution in English can be found in volume 2 of Amos J. Peaslee, *The Constitutions of Nations* (1965) [1.41].

The role of the United States in this entire period has attracted considerable foreign and Italian attention. Four of the more recent additions to this literature cover the ground comprehensively: John Lamberton Harper, *America and the Reconstruction of Italy, 1945-48* (1986) [1.35]; James Edward Miller, *The United States and Italy, 1940-1950* (1986) [1.40]; Timothy Smith, *The United States, Italy and NATO 1947-1952* (1991) [1.44]; and R. Quartararo, *Italia e Stati Uniti. Gli anni difficili (1945-1952)* (1986) [1.42]. All deal with the central question of the extent to which countries such as Italy were able to exercise independent control over their reconstruction. They confirm the conventional wisdom that the thrust of U.S. policy in this period was to support those forces and parties which offered the best opportunity of consolidating capitalism and liberal democracy in Italy against the threat of communism and a possible insurrection. The closest Italy actually came to an attempted insurrection was after an assassination attempt on the leader of the Italian Communist Party (PCI), Palmiro Togliatti, in July

1948, Togliatti forbidding any such adventurism from his hospital bed. The story is told in Walter Tobagi, *La rivoluzione impossibile: l'attentato a Togliatti — violenza politica e reazione popolare* (1978) [1.46].

1950s-1960s

There are few general books which specifically cover the 1950s and Cold War Italy or both decades (1950s and 1960s) in one volume. Exceptions are Christopher Duggan and Christopher Wagstaffe (eds), *Italy in the Cold War. Politics, Culture and Society, 1945-1958* (1995) [1.50], and AA.VV, *Il miracolo economico e il centro-sinistra* (1990) [1.48]. Themes such as the economic miracle (Giorgio Bocca, *Il miracolo italiano* (1980) [1.49] and Eugenio Scalfari, *Rapporto sul neo-capitalismo in Italia* (1961) [1.55]) and the consolidation of Christian Democratic power (see Chapter 2) have figured prominently in research and are relevant for the 1960s too (and the Centre-Left experiment). One of the themes unique to the 1950s was the agrarian reform on which Russell King, *Land Reform: The Italian Experience* (1973) [1.51] provides a useful overview. Perhaps the most stimulating work on this period is Sidney Tarrow, *Peasant Communism in Southern Italy* (1967) [1.56] which analyzes the agrarian reform in a way which enlightens the history of the Italian Communist Party, the Christian Democrats and the politics of the south in the 1950s.

The experience of the Tambroni government (July 1960) marked an important turning point in Italian politics, revealing, as it did, the unacceptability of any government coalition based on the support of the neo-Fascists (Piergiuseppe Murgia, *Il luglio 1960* (1960) [1.53]). It also made entry of the Socialist Party into government (the 'opening to the left') more likely, and the 1960s (until 1968) became dominated by the Centre-Left experiment, which is best documented in Giuseppe Tamburrano, *Storia e cronaca della centro-sinistra* (1971) [1.57], and the debate over its goals, achievement and significance, which is best illustrated in Valentino Parlato (ed), *Spazio e ruolo del riformismo* (1974) [1.54]. The entry of the PSI into government was predicated on the belief that structural changes were possible to achieve in advanced capitalism due to the emergence of an interventionist state and a system of planning. Economic planning was the political catchword in the late 1950s and 1960s, and Italian attempts (and their failure) are usefully analysed in Joseph La Palombara, *Italy: The Politics of Planning* (1966) [1.52]. The failure of the Centre-Left was a partial cause of the social and political militancy of the late 1960s which has been subject to considerable research and is analyzed in chapters 4 and 5.

1970s-1990s

The two major collections which focus specifically on Italy's crisis in the 1970s (Luigi Graziano and Sidney Tarrow (eds), *La crisi italiana* (1979) [1.73] and Fabio Luca Cavazza and Stephen R. Graubard (eds), *Il caso italiano. Italia anni '70* (1975) [1.67]) have not been translated in their complete form, despite their quality and having been products of transatlantic cooperation. Of similar quality is AA.VV, *Nuovi equilibri e nuove prospettivi* (1990) [1.58] which analyses the decade from a broad perspective and includes chapters on terrorism, regionalism, the economy, the mass media, trade unions, the church, parties and electoral competition. Antonio Lombardo (ed), *Il sistema disintegrato. Il sistema politico italiano tra sviluppi e crisi (1974-77)* (1977) [1.75] focuses on the period leading up to and including the beginning of the Historic

Compromise (when the PCI supported, through its abstention, the continuance of the DC in office on the basis of a programmatic accord). The strategies of the parties in this critical period are analysed by Giancarlo Lupi, *Il crollo della grande coalizione: la strategia delle elites dei partiti (1976-1979)* (1982) [1.76]. The commonly-recognised 'low-point' in the history of the Republic was the kidnapping and murder of the Christian Democrat leader Aldo Moro in 1978. The best accounts of this episode are: Mimmo Scarano and Maurizio De Luca, *Il mandarino è marcio* (1985) [1.78] which attempts to unravel the ambiguous role of the secret services in the affair; Giorgio Bocca, *Moro: una tragedia italiana* (1978) [1.61] which reproduces most of Moro's famous prison letters; and Robin Erica Wagner-Pacifici, *The Moro Morality Play. Terrorism as Social Drama* (1986) [1.81] which adopts an unconventional dramaturgic approach.

The breaking of the FIAT strike in 1980 constituted a watershed in the history of Italian political economy and marked a significant change in industrial relations for the next decade (A. Baldissera, *La rivolta dei quarantamila: Dai quadri FIAT ai COBAS* (1988) [1.59]). A detailed historical work of the 1980s has not yet appeared, although there are two good edited volumes on Italy in the 1980s and 1990s. Fabio Luca Cavazza (ed), *La riconquista dell'Italia. Economia. Istituzioni. Politica* (1993) [1.68] is designed to be a follow-up volume to *Il caso italiano* [1.67], and proceeds on the assumption that the anomalies at the heart of the Italian crisis identified by the earlier volume are being overcome. The book ranges across politics, economics and society and includes analysis and prescriptions (some of which have inevitably become dated) from academics and political participants. Paul Ginsborg (ed), *Stato dell'Italia* (1994) [1.72] is quite a remarkable production. It brings together 130 authors and has 180 contributions in 704 pages including 90 pages of statistics. It is genuinely interdisciplinary and is deservedly entitled 'state of Italy'. The contributions are inevitably shorter than usual, but they are of a succinct academic nature and contain short, selective bibliographic guides. There is also a good account of the Italian economy and society in the 1980s by Renato Brunetta, *Il modello Italia. Analisi e chronache degli anni ottanta* (1991) [1.63]. The remarkable success of the Italian economy in these years, often referred to as the 'second economic miracle' has been analysed in Giuseppe Turani, *1985-1995. Il secondo miracolo economico italiano* (1986) [1.80] (although the ten year prognosis was somewhat optimistic).

The dramatic changes in the late 1980s and early 1990s (a product of a combination of national and international factors, and particularly the collapse of Communism in eastern Europe and the exposure of corruption in Italy) have created a new agenda for research, but one which is still in its infancy. A multitude of 'instant histories', analyses and prognoses have appeared on what has been described as the end of the first republic and the beginning of the second, but the large majority of them are too journalistic and lack historical perspective. An exception to this is Massimo L. Salvadori, *Storia d'Italia e crisi di un regime: alle radici della politica italiana* (1994) [1.77], which attempts to explain the crisis of the 1990s in the context of continuity with the past, and specifically the failure to achieve alternation in government. Other works of note on the most recent period are: Luciano Cafagna, *La grande slavina. L'Italia verso la crisi* (1993) [1.65]; Mauro Calise, *Dopo la partitocrazia. L'Italia tra modelli e realtà* (1995) [1.66]; Alberto Benzoni and Roberto Gritti, *La terra di nessuno. Alla ricerca della Repubblica perduta* (1995) [1.60]; Massimo Teodori, *Una nuova Repubblica? Il voto e la riforma elettorale, il tramonto dei partiti, la questione del governo nella democrazia dell'alternanza* (1994) [1.79]; Mark Gilbert, *The Italian Revolution. The Ignominious End of Politics, Italian Style* (1995) [1.71]; and Paolo De Lalla Millal, *Topografia politica della Seconda Repubblica. 1. La Destra* (1994) [1.69], which is the first volume in what will be a series on the collapse of the old order and the rise of new political forces. Michael Braun,

L'Italia da Andreotti a Berlusconi. Rivolgimenti e prospettive politiche in un paese a rischio (1995) [1.62] provides a succinct historical overview.

The best overall analysis of this most recent period from a political science perspective is Mario Caciagli, Franco Cazzola, Leonardo Morlino and Stefano Passigli (eds), *L'Italia fra crisi e transizione* (1994) [1.64] which brings together Italy's best political scientists and sociologists to analyses Italy's transition. Its equivalent in English is Stephen Gundle and Simon Parker (eds), *The New Italian Republic. From the Fall of Communism to the Rise of Berlusconi* (1995) [1.74] which brings together more than fifteen specialists from Italy, Britain and North America to analyse Italy's transition between 1989 and 1994. The other works of quality produced on this period are those devoted to electoral change, on which see Chapter 2 (section on voting behaviour). There have also been some works on corruption in the 1990s, on which see Chapter 2 (section on clientelism and corruption). A final book worth mentioning, the transcript of a discussion, is Vittorio Foa, Paul Ginsborg et al., *Le virtù della Repubblica. Dalla crisi del sistema e dal ricambio della classe politica lo spazio per una nuova cultura di governo* (1994) [1.70]. The contributors include a number of significant observers and activists and the discussion is a wide ranging one on the current state of the Italian Republic, its past and likely future. Even though the discussion rapidly dated (Berlusconi is hardly mentioned, for example), it contains a number of important and stimulating observations which are worth reading.

BIOGRAPHIES, MEMOIRS, SPEECHES, WRITINGS

One of the Italian political system's enduring characteristics is the stability and continuity of its top political personnel (which contrasts with the instability and short-lived nature of its governments). The average political life of an Italian politician is much longer than, say, his or her British counterpart, and several leading politicians of the immediate postwar period were still prominent in the 1980s, a few (such as Andreotti) even in the early 1990s. These individuals have had a considerable influence on the character and operation of the Italian political system. Unfortunately, however, despite (or perhaps because of) this long tenure, writing about government from first hand experience has not proved to be a popular past-time. There are few worthy memoirs or autobiographies of postwar ministers and civil servants which, in countries like Britain, have proved to be significant resources for those conducting research into the complex processes of government.

Exceptions to this trend include the diaries of the ex-leader of the PSI, Pietro Nenni, *Diari* (1981-83) [1.101]; those of Mariano Rumor (edited by E. Reato and Francesco Malgeri), *Memorie (1943-1970)* (1991) [1.104], ex-leader of the DC and of the powerful Dorotei faction, five times Prime Minister and someone who just avoided standing trial for the Lockheed scandal; and those of Antonio Giolitti, *Lettere a Marta. Ricordi e riflessioni* (1992) [1.92], the ex-communist who left the PCI in 1956 to become a socialist and eventually the Minister of the Budget in the first Centre-Left government in December 1963. Mention should also be made of the autobiography of Vittorio Foa, *Il cavallo e la torre. Riflessioni su una vita* (1991) [1.90], the influential ex-leader of the CGIL (see Chapter 4, section on labour market and interest groups) and left wing socialists who led many trade union activists out of the PSI and into the PSIUP in 1964 (see Chapter 2, section on political parties: individual studies).

Another source of the thoughts and interpretations of key political and social actors is the *Intervista...* series run by the publishing house Laterza. The books constitute in-depth interviews with either leading academics or political and economic elites. They become, in time, useful historical sources. A few examples will suffice to give a flavour of the series: Luciano Lama, *Intervista sul sindacato* (1976) [1.95]; Giulio Andreotti, *Intervista su De Gasperi* (1977) [1.82]; Guido Carli, *Intervista sul capitalismo italiano* (1977) [1.84]; Pietro Nenni, *Intervista sul socialismo italiano* (1977) [1.100]; and Pasquale Saraceno, *Intervista sulla ricostruzione 1943-1953* (1977) [1.106]. The most interesting book in English which relates first-hand experiences of postwar politics is Furio Colombo (ed), *In Italy. Post War Political Life: interviews with Andreotti, Nenni, Terracini, Spriano, La Malfa, Lama, Saraceno, Carli.* (1981) [1.85].

The shortage of good memoirs has also made biographies less 'complete' than they might otherwise be. Nevertheless, there are some biographical accounts of leading politicians which provide good insights into the working of the political system and the nature of postwàr political life: Pietro Scoppola, *La proposta politica di De Gasperi* (1977) [1.108], first leader of the DC, eight times Prime Minister (consecutively between 1945 and 1953) and the dominant force shaping Italian politics in the immediate postwar period; Giorgio Galli, *Fanfani* (1975) [1.91], ex-leader of the Christian Democrats (DC), six times Prime Minster, a key figure in the changes the DC underwent in the 1950s and one of the longest-standing influential politicians in the postwar period; Gino Pallotta, *Andreotti, il Richelieu della politica italiana* (1988) [1.102], Christian Democrat, seven times Prime Minister and probably the most influential politician in the postwar period until he was placed under judicial investigation in 1993 for possible collusion with the mafia; Giorgio Bocca, *Togliatti* (1977) [1.83], ex-leader of the Italian Communist Party (PCI) and the person primarily responsible for turning the PCI into a mass party in the postwar period; Enzo Santarelli, *Nenni* (1993) [1.105], the inspiration of postwar Italian socialism; Miriam Mafai, *L'uomo che sognava la lotta armata* (1984) [1.98], the story of Pietro Secchia, Togliatti's chief source of opposition from orthodox stalinists inside the PCI in the 1950s; Aniellio Coppola, *Moro* (1976) [1.86], ex-leader of the DC, five times Prime Minister and the politician who attempted to fashion a compromise between the DC and the PCI and was kidnapped and murdered by the Red Brigades in 1978 (see section on 1970s-1990s above);   Chiara Valentini, *Berlinguer. Il Segretario* (1990) [1.110], ex-leader of the PCI (in the 1970s and early 1980s), who took the party to its postwar electoral peak in 1976, was strategist of the Historic Compromise (DC-PCI agreement) in the mid-1970s and was responsible for breaking the PCI's link with Moscow in 1981 (over the *coup* in Poland); Mino Lorusso, *Occhetto. Il comunismo italiano da Togliatti al PDS* (1992) [1.97], last leader of the PCI and responsible for its transformation into the Democratic Party of the Left (PDS); Primo di Nicola, *Mario Segni* (1992) [1.88], ex-Christian Democrat and son of the former President Antonio Segni (1962-4), protagonist of institutional reforms and reform of the DC which he left in 1993 to concentrate on building a new political movement, Alleanza Democratica (Democratic Alliance). Short biographical sketches are provided in *Dizionario biografico degli italiani* (1960-) [1.89] and in Frank Coppa, *Dictionary of Modern Italian History* [1.4].

Other useful resources for the historian are collections of the writings and speeches of leading politicians. Complete collections (i.e. of politicians who are retired or dead) are rare. Antonio Gramsci, *Opere* (1970-) [1.93] and Palmiro Togliatti, *Opere* (1973-) [1.109] are exceptions. Other useful collections are: Maria Romana De Gasperi (ed), *De Gasperi scrive. Corrispondenza con capi di stato, cardinali, uomini politici, giornalisti, diplomatici* (1974) [1.87]; Pier Giorgio Zunino (ed), *Scritti politici di Alcide De Gasperi* (1979) [1.111]; Ferrucio Parri (edited by E. Collotti, G. Rochat, G. Solaro Pelazza, R. Speziale), *Scritti 1915/1975* (1976) [1.103] (Parri was leader of the short-lived Action Party and briefly prime Minister during the postwar settlement); Ugo La Malfa (edited by Giancarlo Tartaglia), *Scritti 1925-1953* (1988) [1.94]; Riccardo Lombardi (edited by

Simona Colarizzi), *Scritti politici, 1945-1978* (1978) [1.96]; Giuseppe Saragat, *Quarant'anni di lotta per la democrazia. Scritti e discorsi 1925-1965* (1966) [1.107]; and Aldo Moro, *L'intelligenza e gli avvenimenti. Testi 1959-1978* (1979) [1.99].

Short collections of speeches and writings of active politicians are far more numerous, especially of politicians of the left. These are published rapidly and are often directed as much towards party members (engaged in internal factional struggles) as the outside world. The authors are often recognised leaders of factions, and the books consequently become useful sources of the history of a party's internal politics. The profusion of books by Giorgio Amendola, Giorgio Napolitano and Pietro Ingrao (PCI faction leaders in the 1960s and 1970s) are exemplary, but, with others, are too numerous to list here.

NOTES

1.   Indeed, they have been compared by the authors themselves in an illuminating Roundtable discussion, later published in *Passato e Presente*, a. XI (1993), n. 29, May-August, pp.11-32.

2.   The publication of the book in 1991 produced a veritable flood of reviews, debates and articles in Italian periodicals which are too numerous to cite here, but which confirm the book's significance to the history of the Resistance.

2

Politics

GENERAL WORKS[1]

Encouraging more research on Italian politics and government has been considerably hampered by the scarcity of basic textbooks. The legalistic orientation of basic texts (best expressed in English by John Clarke Adams and Paolo Barile, *The Government of Republican Italy* (1972) [2.3]) was overcome only in the early 1970s with books by Percy Allum, *Italy. Republic Without Government?* [2.4], Raphael Zariski, *Italy. The Politics of Uneven Development* (1972) [2.24], and Paolo Farneti (ed), *Il sistema politico italiano* (1973) [2.11]. Subsequently, however, no texts were published for over ten years and no amended editions of the earlier texts were made.

This glaring gap has been partially rectified in recent years. There are now three standard (but very different) textbooks in English: Donald Sassoon, *Contemporary Italy. Politics, Economics and Society since 1945* (1986) [2.21]; Frederic Spotts and Theodor Weiser, *Italy. A Difficult Democracy* (1986) [2.22]; and David Hine, *Governing Italy: The Politics of Bargained Pluralism* (1993) [2.13]. Sassoon's is not a conventional student text book. Indeed, the author himself argues that the book is neither political science, sociology, history nor economics. He structures the book in three parts - the economy, society and politics - and attempts to unravel the complex relationship between them to give a detailed picture of postwar Italy. The book is based on a wealth of Italian literature and statistics and has a large (but unsectioned) bibliography. Political scientists may feel that, despite protestations to the contrary in the introduction, Sassoon's scenario does not give enough emphasis to politics and particularly, in a system characterised by 'party rule', to the political parties.

Italy. A Difficult Democracy [2.22] is a more conventional text written by a German journalist and a former member of the American Diplomatic Service. They seek to explain how and why the political system (despite defects which logically should destroy it) not only survives but functions reasonably well. Inevitably, the book is rather journalistic in style. The authors do not use theoretical arguments and frameworks (which would clarify their essential thesis), their grasp of history is minimal, and there are no footnotes (although there is a useful select bibliography).

Governing Italy: The Politics of Bargained Pluralism [2.13] is the most solid and well written textbook available. The author adopts a primarily institutional focus in explaining the nature of political system (which he characterises as 'bargained, multi-tiered, juridicized pluralism') and why it is difficult to reform. This focus is welcome in view of the absence of good studies in English of Italy's formal institutional framework. As a consequence, however, other political and socio-economic themes are treated rather superficially making it difficult to view this as a comprehensive textbook of Italian politics.

The beginner in Italian studies will also gain from the section by Stephen Hellman in Mark Kesselman et al., *European Politics in Transition* (1992) [2.14], which provides useful introductory material on the Italian political system and, with other countries analysed in the same book, allows the reader to view the system in a comparative context. A similar introductory comparative treatment is provided in Italian by Zeffiro Ciuffoletti and Serge Noiret (eds), *I modelli di democrazia in Europa e il caso italiano* (1992) [2.9]. Mark Donovan (ed), *Italy* (1996) [2.10] is a useful resource for both teachers and students of Italian politics. It reproduces approximately twenty five key journal articles on Italian politics and government. The book is structured around several sections and the editor's selection is primarily articles published in the 1980s and 1990s, so it should have long term use value. Giorgio Bocca, *La disunità d'Italia* (1990) [2.7] is an example of how journalistic incisiveness can provide a useful introduction to the contemporary Italian political scene.

Several general books of a less introductory nature should be mentioned. Sidney Tarrow and Peter Lange (eds), *Italy in Transition. Conflict and Consensus* (1979) [2.23], is an important milestone in the study of Italian politics and remains indispensable reading for those wishing to understand Italy in the period until the end of the 1970s. The editors sought to challenge those authors who stressed the uniqueness of Italian politics by providing data and analyses to make the Italian case more accessible and comprehensible to comparativists. Martin J. Bull and Martin Rhodes (eds), *Transition and Crisis in Italian Politics* (1996) [2.8] picks up, to some extent, where Tarrow and Lange left off. This collection brings together several key specialists to analyse the changes which Italian politics underwent in the 1980s and 1990s, with a view to locating the dramatic changes of the 1990s in firmer historical context. The collection of articles in Gianfranco Pasquino (ed), *Il Sistema Politico Italiano* (1985) [2.19] provides in depth analyses of various areas by subject specialists. *Lezioni sull'Italia repubblicana* (1994) [2.5] is a multi-authored work by Piero Bevilacqua, Carlo Carboni, Fabio Levi, Salvatore Lupo, Rosario Mangiameli, Claudio Pavone, Nicola Tranfaglia and Carlo Triglia. It evaluates the experience of the Italian Republic from a number of angles. Part of the book has a chronological perspective and part a thematic perspective. Paul Furlong, *Modern Italy. Representation and Reform* (1994) [3.100] is primarily about policy-making (see Chapter 3, section on policy-making), but also serves as a general text.

Joseph LaPalombara, *Democracy Italian Style* (1987) [2.16] is one of the most lively and controversial books to be published on Italy in recent years (in redefining Italy as a model of stable democracy) and should be read for that reason alone. His essential thesis is that Italian democracy not only performs in a far more successful manner than is usually presumed (something which is not that controversial amongst Italian specialists, but remains in stark contrast with a vast amount of literature produced on Italy in the 1970s), but is, in fact, a strong and stable democracy which is highly participatory and has fostered a deep sense of commitment amongst its people towards democratic government. The strength of the political system, it is argued, derives from its adaptability and flexibility, qualities which would be undermined by the introduction of institutional reforms. As expected, the book has had a mixed reception amongst Italianists. Several criticisms have been levelled against it, perhaps the most important being the author's failure to root his analysis in a comparative context (even an implicit one) which would allow a proper evaluation of the Italian experience.[2] It might be added that his book has become dated by events of the early 1990s. The discovery (through judicial action) of the extent of corruption which had upheld the ruling parties' power, the public's widespread reaction to this exposure and the achievement of institutional reform all make LaPalombara's interpretation less convincing. Indeed, some may see it as an apologia for some of the system's worst practices. Certainly, the books already cited above paint a more complex picture of political practice and change.

Finally, of important general texts, mention should be made of Robert Putnam (with Robert Leonardi and Raffaella Nanetti), *Making Democracy Work. Civic Traditions in Modern Italy* (1992) [2.20]. This book draws on over a decade of survey analysis of Italian regional governments as a means of explaining institutional performance. Putnam and his colleagues evaluate the performance of the regional governments (in terms of the delivery of services to the population) against several criteria. The league table established by this exercise is unsurprising in that the governments in the South consistently do less well than those in the North. Yet, the explanation for this difference does break new ground. Putnam finds no consistent correlation between the degree of economic development and the more successful regional governments. On the contrary, the variations between the performance of different regional governments is best explained by the presence or not of a civic culture, a distinct phenomenon which encourages networks of integrated support inspired by trust. Putnam subsequently explains the presence of this civic culture in terms of Italy's particular pattern of historical development over eight centuries. *Making Democracy Work* is a seminal contribution to the study of Italy and, more generally, to the study of institutions, explaining, as it does, institutional performance in terms of an area's historically-determined cultural assets.

Two yearbooks provide essential material on current events for those studying Italian politics. *Italian Politics: A Review* (1986-) [2.1] (with a translated version, *Politica in Italia. I fatti dell'anno e le interpretazioni* [2.2]) was launched in 1986 through the efforts of the Cattaneo Institute and has had various editors. The volumes bring together different specialists who analyse the previous year's main political issues and events. Ruud Koole and Peter Mair (eds), *Political Data Yearbook* (1992-) [2.15] is a comparative yearbook which was launched in 1992 and provides a more synthetic account of the previous year's events in one chapter. Gino Palotta, *Dizionario della politica italiana* (1985) [2.18] provides a useful guide to the complexities of Italian politics. For those interested in the work of Italian political scientists, Luigi Graziano (ed), *La scienza politica in Italia: bilancio e prospettive* (1986) [2.12], and Leonardo Morlino (ed), *Scienza Politica* (1989) [2.17], are good resources, particularly the latter. Finally, Norberto Bobbio, *Saggi sulla scienza politica in Italia* (1971) [2.6] provides a select, but excellent treatment of some of the theories of the founders of Italian political science.

POLITICAL PARTIES AND THE PARTY SYSTEM: GENERAL STUDIES

A useful introductory text on Italian political parties which also contains a good bibliography is Simona Colarizzi, *Storia dei partiti nell'Italia repubblicana* (1994) [2.25]. For the basic statistical and organizational data on Italian political parties there is nothing to compare with Richard Katz and Peter Mair (eds), *Party Organizations in Western Democracies 1960-1990* (two volumes) (1992-93) [2.31]. The chapter in the first volume by Luciano Bardi and Leonardo Morlino provides data of considerable breadth and depth on Italian parties (over 161 pages), and it is impressively supported with an explanatory chapter in the second volume. It is an indispensable reference work.

The importance of Giorgio Galli and Alfonso Prandi, *Patterns of Political Participation in Italy* [2.28] to the study of parties in Italy has already been noted (in the Introduction above). The importance of the debate over interpretations of the party system was also noted, and reference made to the two main interpretations: 'polarised pluralism' by Giovanni Sartori, in his work *Parties and Party Systems: A Framework for Analysis* (1976) [2.37], usefully summarised in *Teoria dei partiti e caso italiano* (1982) [2.38]; and an 'imperfect two-party system' by Giorgio Galli, in his work *Il bipartitismo imperfetto. Comunisti e democristiani in Italia* [2.29], which has been expanded and up-dated in *I partiti politici italiani, 1943-1991. Dalla Resistenza all'Europa integrata* (1992) [2.30].

A further interpretation was developed by Paolo Farneti in *The Italian Party System* (1985) [2.27], a work which, after Farneti's sudden death, was finished posthumously by several people under the guidance of the Dutch political scientist, Hans Daalder. Even though one detects the work's unfinished nature (as a single-authored product) the book provides a good summary of the social bases of the parties, the nature of their interactions and their individual organisations and ideologies. His interpretation of 'centripetal pluralism' empirically rejects Sartori's thesis that centrifugal drives are at the heart of the Italian party system. The book provides the best account available in English of the political parties and the party system. Also worth reading, although now a little dated, is Giuseppe Tamburrano, *Pci e Psi nel sistema democristiano* (1978) [2.39], which analyses the parties within the context of the broader political system.

Specifically on the internal nature of the parties, Giovanni Sartori, *Correnti, frazioni e fazioni nei partiti politici italiani* (1973) [2.36] is to be recommended. Comparative (as opposed to single-party) work produced in the 1980s focused on the parties' organisational decline and attempts at internal reform. C. Vallauri (ed), *I partiti italiani tra declino e riforma* (1986) [2.40] covers a wide range of ground, and Gianfranco Pasquino, *Degenerazioni e riforme dei partiti* (1982) [2.34] offers an illuminating and critical insider's view of the parties' malfunctioning. The financing of parties and their growing deficits has long been a controversial issue (state financing was abolished in a referendum in April 1993) and is analyzed in Giorgio Pacifici, *Il costo della democrazia: i partiti italiani attraverso i loro bilanci* (1983) [2.32], and Cleoffe Corona, *Il costo della democrazia: i partiti politici italiani, costi e finanziamenti* (1984) [2.26]. Understanding the origins and nature of governing coalitions is crucial to understanding the dynamics of the Italian party system and the political system as a whole. Geoffrey Pridham, *Political Parties and Coalition Behaviour in Italy* (1988) [2.35] is the only book length text in English which analyses the complexities of Italian coalition behaviour. He adopts an inductive approach, analysing the Italian case in its own right rather than according to the postulation of certain assumptions which, in the Italian case, do not hold. The book is unnecessarily long, but does contain a wealth of information for those interested in this subject area.

POLITICAL PARTIES: INDIVIDUAL STUDIES

Italian Communism (PCI/PDS, PDUP, RC)

The Italian Communist Party (*Partito comunista italiano*, PCI), from the perspective of having been permanently in opposition, must rank as one of the most over-studied parties in western Europe. Books in the 1960s by Donald Blackmer (*Unity in Diversity. Italian Communism and the Communist World* (1968) [2.44]) and Sidney Tarrow (*Peasant Communism in Southern Italy* [1.56]), set the trend for scholarly research, but it was their pioneering edited volume, *Communism in Italy and France* (1975) [2.45], which acted as a major stimulus to empirical and theoretical research in a national and international context.

The two most comprehensive works on the party remain untranslated. The vast 800 page volume, Renato Mieli (ed), *Il PCI allo specchio. Venticinque anni di storia del comunismo italiano* (1983) [2.55] brings together a number of specialists who analyse the party along a number of thematic dimensions. Each chapter is accompanied by a research report and useful bibliography. Aris Accornero et al., *L'identità comunista, i militanti, le strutture, la cultura del PCI* (1983) [2.41] is probably the most thorough sociological study of a political party in Italy, based as it is on a survey of 16,000 delegates to the PCI's provincial congresses in 1979. Massimo Ilardi and Aris Accornero (eds), *Il Partito comunista italiano: struttura e storia dell'organizzazione* (1982) [2.52] is a useful collection of articles on the history and organisation of the party.

A straightforward comparative history of the two main parties of the left is provided by Alexander De Grand, *The Italian Left in the Twentieth Century: A History of the Socialist and Communist Parties* (1989) [2.75]. Donald Sassoon, *The Strategy of the Italian Communist Party. From the Resistance to the Historic Compromise* (1981) [2.56] provides a rather sympathetic account of the PCI's (primarily early) postwar strategy (or at least what the leadership claimed was party strategy). Grant Amyot, *The Italian Communist Party. The Crisis of the Popular Front Strategy* (1981) [2.42] analyses the fundamental divisions and debate inside the party in the 1950s and 1960s (and specifically the Amendola-Ingrao dispute) both at the national and local levels. The continued recalcitrance of some members of the extreme left of the party (organised into the Manifesto Group) led to their eventual expulsion in the late 1960s (although Ingrao stayed in the party) and the formation of a new party, the Democratic Party of Proletarian Unity (PDUP) (some of whose members eventually returned to the PCI in the mid-1980s, others of whom joined Proletarian Democracy (DP)). PDUP's story is told in Aldo Garzia, *Da Natta a Natta. Storia del Manifesto e del PDUP* (1985) [2.48].

Silvano Belligni (ed), *La giraffa e il liocorno. Il Pci dagli anni '70 al nuovo decennio* (1983) [2.43] contains several good analyses of the party's behaviour in the 1970s at both the national and sub-national levels. Joan Barth Urban, *Moscow and the Italian Communist Party* (1986) [2.58] unravels the complex development of the PCI's autonomy from Moscow through the use of a wealth of primary material (although it is a pity that greater space in the book is not devoted to the most recent period). Stephen Hellman, *Italian Communism in Transition. The Rise and Fall of the Historic Compromise in Turin, 1975-1980* (1988) [2.50] brilliantly portrays a party undergoing crisis and change by focusing on the fate of the Historic Compromise strategy in Turin. This last work provides an essential backdrop to understanding the changes the party subsequently went through in the 1980s. On the party's transformation into the Democratic Party of the Left (PDS), a succinct and thoughtful analysis is provided by Piero Ignazi, *Dal PCI al PDS* (1992) [2.51]. The party's decision to change itself into a non-communist party of the left led to a split of a minority of far left members who created a new communist party, *Rifondazione comunista* (Reconstructed Communism). It is still too early for any substantial work to have been completed on this party, but useful reflections on its birth are provided by its first leader, Sergio Garavini, in *Le ragioni di un comunista. Scritti e riflessioni sullo scioglimento del Pci e sulla nascita di una nuova forza comunista in Italia* (1991) [2.47].

Mention should also be made of Paolo Spriano, *Storia del Partito Comunista* (1967-1975) [2.57] (5 volumes), even though only the final volume deals with the immediate postwar period. This is the official history of the PCI written by the party's leading historian. Accepting the limitations of an insider's history, the work is a major contribution to the history of the party. It is rich in sources and insights and is based on a wealth of original documentation and personal experience. It is also probably the best work in any language to provide a clear idea and sense of what it was like to be a communist in western Europe in the pre-war and immediate postwar period. Historians of the party can now benefit from the first volume (covering the period of the Constituent

Assembly, 1946-1948) of the PCI's previously confidential leadership discussions: Renzo Martinelli and Maria Luisa Righi (eds), *La politica del Partito comunista italiano nel periodo costituente. I verbali della direzione tra il V e il VI Congresso 1946-1948* (1992) [2.54].

Finally, although this research guide does not cover social and political theory, mention should be made of Antonio Gramsci, one of the founding members of the PCI, its first leader and the most famous Marxist theorist Italy has produced. Reading Gramsci is necessary for anyone seeking a full understanding of the postwar history of the PCI simply because of the claims made by the postwar leadership that party strategy was primarily shaped by his political thought, and specifically by the notebooks that he produced in the 1930s in a fascist prison (where he subsequently died). The best edition of the notebooks in English is edited (and translated) by Quinton Hoare and Geoffrey Nowell-Smith: Antonio Gramsci, *Selections from the Prison Notebooks* (1971) [2.49]. Joseph Femia, *Gramsci's Political Thought: Hegemony, Consciousness and the Revolutionary Process* (1981) [2.46] provides a good synthesis of, and commentary on, Gramsci's political thought. For the uninitiated, James Joll, *Gramsci* (1978) [2.53] is a good introduction to Gramsci's life and writings.

Christian Democracy (DC)

Works on Italian Christian Democracy (*Democrazia cristiana*, DC) are less abundant than those on the PCI, particularly in English. An early, rather sympathetic (and hardly rigorous), account is found in Mario Einaudi and Francois Goguel (eds), *Christian Democracy in Italy and France* (1969) [2.62]. The best and most recent overview for the beginner is provided by Robert Leonardi and Douglas Wertman, *Italian Christian Democracy: The Politics of Dominance* (1989) [2.66], but a comprehensive narrative history of the party in English has still to be written.

For the DC specialist the official history of the party is now complete: Francesco Malgeri (ed), *Storia della Democrazia Cristiana* (1978-1989) [2.68] (5 volumes). The two volumes produced on the period 1945-1962 by the Catholic political scientist Gianni Baget-Bozzo should also be mentioned for their richness in historical detail: *Il Partito Cristiano al Potere. La DC di De Gasperi e di Dossetti 1945-1954* (1974) [2.59], and *Il Partito Cristiano e l'apertura a sinistra. La DC di Fanfani e di Moro 1954-1962* (1977) [2.60]. A more digestible account is Giorgio Galli, *Mezzo secolo di DC 1943-1993. Da De Gasperi a Mario Segni* (1993) [2.65] which brings together and up-dates the author's earlier work on the party. He attempts to explain the origins of the DC's hegemony and the party's identity, and in doing so looks not only at the behaviour of the DC itself but also the attitudes and behaviour of the left.

Franco Cassano, *Il teorema democristiana. La mediazione della Dc nella società e nel sistema politico italiano* (1979) [2.61] is an important contribution to the debate on the exact nature, or identity, of the DC. Rejecting Galli's view that the DC is a party representative of the 'state bourgeoisie' (serviced through the extensive state sector of the economy), Cassano argues that, rather than representing interests, the DC's nature is simply the product of its permanence in power and of the reasons for that permanence (the 'anti-system' nature of the only alternative, the PCI). Hence, the production of policies in government which cannot be identified with those of a genuine conservative party.

Other general works of quality on the party are Arturo Parisi (ed), *Democristiani* (1979) [2.69], and, on the party' difficulties and decline in the late 1970s and early 1980s, Arrigo Levi, *La DC nell'Italia che cambia* (1984) [2.67]. Alan Zuckerman, *The Politics of Faction: Christian Democratic Rule in Italy* (1979) [2.71] is essential reading in order to understand the internal nature and dynamics of the DC. Giancarlo Provasi, *Borghesia industriale e Democrazia cristiana. Sviluppo economico e mediazione politica dalla ricostruzione agli anni '70* (1976) [2.70] explores the fractious and changing relationship between the DC and Italian business elites. Two recent works by the journalist Marco Follini analyse the DC's troubled dominance in the 1980s and its deep crisis in the early 1990s (which eventually led to its break up and relaunch in 1994 as the Italian Popular Party (*Partito popolare* (PPI), the name of the DC's pre-war predecessor): *L'arcipelago democristiano* (1990) [2.63] and *La DC al bivio* (1993) [2.64]. There are several other studies of the DC which have been included in the section on clientelism below.

Italian Socialism (PSI, PSDI, PSIUP)

The most complete history of the Italian Socialist Party (*Partito socialista italiano*, PSI) (up to the end of the 1970s) is the six volume study completed under the direction of Giovanni Sabbatucci, *Storia del socialismo italiano* (1980-81) [2.82], the last two volumes being dedicated to the postwar period. The most up to date history of the party in the postwar period is Zeffiro Ciuffoletti, Maurizio Degli'Innocenti, Giovanni Sabbatucci, *Storia del Psi. III. Dal Dopoguerra a oggi* (1993) [2.74], which is the third of a three-volume history. Good histories of the party in one volume include Giorgio Galli, *Storia del socialismo italiano* (1980) [2.77], and Antonio Landolfi, *Storia del Psi. Cent'anni di socialismo in Italia da Filippo Turati a Bettino Craxi* (1990) [2.78]. Spencer Di Scala, *Renewing Italian Socialism: From Nenni to Craxi* (1988) [2.76] is the only complete history (although uneven in its coverage of some periods) of the PSI available in English. It covers the period from the 1930s until the Craxi period and is based on a wealth of primary sources. It has been criticised for its anti-communist line in dealing with the relations between the PSI and PCI. Better on the changing relations between those parties is Alexander De Grand, *The Italian Left in the Twentieth Century: A History of the Socialist and Communist Parties* [2.75] which begins with the origins of the socialist movement and finishes in 1979.

Francesca Taddei, *Il socialismo italiano del dopoguerra: correnti ideologiche e scelte politiche (1943-1947)* (1984) [2.83] focuses on the postwar settlement which was crucial to the history of Italian socialism because it produced an important split in January 1947 and the birth of the small Italian Social Democratic Party (PSDI). The PSDI is a party on which there has been no research of any substance, although Attilio Tempestini, *Il terzaforzista recidivio. Le linee e i risultati elettorali dei socialdemocratici e dei socialisti da Palazzo Barberini alle elezioni del 1968* (1975) [2.84] contains useful information. The second major split in postwar Italian socialism occurred over the 'opening to the left'. Those on the left of the PSI who opposed the party's entry into government with the DC (to form the Centre-Left) deserted the party and formed the Italian Socialist Party of Proletarian Unity (PSIUP, the pre-war name for the PSI) which lasted until the early 1970s, and the history of which is told by Silvano Miniati, *PSIUP, 1943-72. Vita e morte di un partito* (1981) [2.80].

The transformation of the PSI under its leader, Bettino Craxi, after his appointment in 1976, became one of the key factors in shaping Italian politics during the 1980s. Wolfgang Merkel, *Prima e dopo Craxi: le trasformazioni del Psi* (1987) [2.79] examines the changes in the party under Bettino Craxi. The book has excellent quantitative analyses of the national and local organisations, the social composition of the party membership and electorate, and provides the best analysis of Craxi's rise to power. The same period is also analysed in Paolo Ciofi and Franco Ottaviano, *Un partito per il leader. Il nuovo corso del Psi dal Midas agli anni novanta* (1990) [2.73]. Craxi's fall has yet to be seriously documented, but an 'instant' analysis is provided by Antonio Padellaro, *Processo a Craxi: ascesa e declino di un leader* (1993) [2.81].

As is apparent from this brief survey, the history of Italian socialism is a history of fragmentation, schisms and failed reunification, and research has consequently tended to focus more on narrative history (as a means of documenting these themes) than on organisational and sociological analyses of the parties. Two important exceptions to this trend are the book by Merkel on the party under Craxi mentioned above [2.79] and the older case study by Samuel Barnes, *Party Democracy: Politics in an Italian Socialist Federation* (1967) [2.72] which documents the organisational life of the party federation of Arezzo.

The Other Parties

The parties of the so-called 'laical centre' (which, for many, includes the PSDI referred to above) are virtually devoid of serious political study in book form in English or Italian, apart from the three solid volumes published by the Cattaneo Institute in the 1980s on the Republican Party (PRI): Piergiorgio Corbetta and Arturo Parisi, *Il voto repubblicano alle origini del 26 giugno* (1984) [2.90]; Arturo Parisi and A. Varni (eds), *Organizzazione e politica nel PRI 1946-1984* (1985) [2.103]; and Arturo Parisi (ed), *La dirigenza repubblicana* (1987) [2.104]. Maria Carla Bolla and Giancarlo Trentini, *Il Pri. L'imagine psicosociale di un partito politico* (1983) [2.87] is also a useful study. There has been nothing substantial produced on the Italian Liberal Party (PLI) apart from two histories: Arnaldo Ciani, *Il Partito liberale italiano da Croce a Malagodi* (1968) [2.89], and the more recent Sante Marelli, *Storia dei liberali. Da Cavour a Zanone* (1985) [2.100].

The lack of serious attention to the far right is more surprising in view of its influence on Italian politics and on the dynamics of the Italian party system throughout the postwar period. A couple of studies on the Italian Social Movement (MSI, later MSI-DN: the MSI and the National Right) were produced in the 1970s but are not worthy of mention. Works produced since the late 1980s have made substantial progress in filling this academic gap. Piero Ignazi, *Il polo esclusivo. Profilo del Movimento sociale italiano* (1989) [2.97] is the first serious academic study of the party by a political scientist. Franco Ferraresi, *The Radical Right in Italy* (1988) [2.95] is a more general study of the right. Piero Ignazi, *Postfascisti? Dal Movimento sociale italiano ad Alleanza nazionale* (1995) [2.98] charts the MSI's transformation into a so-called 'post-Fascist' party, the National Alliance (*Alleanza nazionale*, AN) in the 1990s. Finally, Gianni S. Rossi, *Alternative e doppiopetto. Il Msi dalla contestazione alla Destra nazionale (1968-1973)* (1992) [2.105] is a narrowly focused study of the revival of the far right in the early 1970s.

Other small parties have received more attention largely due to their topicality and their attempt to cultivate a different type of political organisation to the traditional political parties. The Radical Party (PR) attracted academic attention in the 1970s, the best analysis being Massimo Teodori, Piero Ignazi and Angelo Panebianco, *I nuovi radicali. Storia e sociologia di un movimento politico* (1977) [2.107]. Walter Veciello (ed), *I radicali. Compagni, qualunquisti, destabilizzatori?* (1981) [2.108] also contains some informative chapters. The Greens likewise attracted attention in the 1980s, particularly as Italy's environmental costs rose with the country's emergence as a leading industrial power. The most useful studies are R. Borcio and G. Lodi, *La sfida verde: il movimento ecologista in Italia* (1988) [2.88], Mario Diani, *Isole nell'arcipelago: il movimento ecologista in Italia* (1988) [2.93], and R. Del Carria, *Il potere diffuso: i Verdi in Italia* (1988) [2.92].

There are several new parties or 'movement-parties' which have risen to prominence in the 1990s as a consequence of the effective meltdown of the old party system. Of these, the two most important are the Northern League and *Forza Italia*. There are two good studies of the former's rise since 1984: Renato Mannheimer, *La Lega Lombarda* (1991) [2.99] and Ilvo Diamanti, *La Lega: geografia, storia e sociologia di un nuovo soggetto politico* (1993) [2.94]. Other books of note are Daniele Vimercati, *I Lombardi alla nuova crociata* (1990) [2.109] and Stefano Allievi, *Le parole della Lega* (1992) [2.85]. *Forza Italia!* (the party set up by the media magnate Silvio Berlusconi in 1994) can hardly be described as small (in view of its 1994 electoral success) but the short period of its existence, coupled with questions about its likely longevity, mean that no scholarly work on the party has yet been produced. There are many journalistic accounts, but most not worthy of academic attention. Alessandro Gilioli, *Forza Italia. La storia, gli uomini, i misteri* (1994) [2.96] is one of the more interesting accounts, and is written by a journalist with the weekly magazine, *L'Europeo*.

Finally, political parties that have existed for brief periods have not been completely unresearched. Books on the PDUP [2.48] and PSIUP [2.80] have already been mentioned above. Gino Pallotta, *Il qualunquismo e l'avventura di Guglielmo Giannini* (1972) [2.102] and Sandro Setta, *L'Uomo qualunque, 1944-1948* (1975) [2.106] explain the rise and fall of the right-wing 'everyman's' party in the immediate postwar period. The document-based *L'Azionismo nella storia d'Italia 1946-1953* (1988) [2.101] (introduced by Lamberto Mercuri) and the exhaustive Giovanni De Luna, *Storia del Partito d'Azione: la rivoluzione democratica: 1942-1947* (1982) [2.91], evaluate the role of the Action Party in the postwar settlement. Luigi Bobbio, *Storia di Lotta Continua* (1979) [2.86] is an extremely good account of the brief life of one of the leading extreme left parties of the 1960s which dissolved in the mid-1970s.[3]

ELECTIONS, VOTING BEHAVIOUR AND REFERENDA

The study of voting behaviour in Italy has long been a major concern, and increasingly the preserve, of Italian sociologists or political scientists with a sociological background. This means that, aside from articles and chapters in edited books and the useful series, *Italy at the Polls* (various years) [2.135] on individual elections edited by Howard Penniman (which currently stops at the 1983 elections), a knowledge of Italian is required for a comprehensive understanding of the psephological debate, the empirical research surrounding which has witnessed a consistent expansion and improvement in quality.

Probably the best general introduction to the area is provided by Renato Mannheimer, *Capire il voto. Contributi per l'analisi del comportamento elettorale in Italia* (1989) [2.126], although several other works listed below are also useful. The general literature on voting behaviour should also be viewed in the broader context of the debate on political culture, of which the classic account is found in the path breaking work by Gabriel Almond and Sidney Verba, *The Civic Culture: Political Attitudes and Democracy in Five Nations* (1963) [2.111]. A good assessment of the impact of this book in Italy and the degree to which portrayal of Italian political culture (as one of political alienation, social isolation and distrust) needs to be modified is found in the chapter by Giacomo Sani in Gabriel Almond and Sidney Verba (eds), *The Civic Culture Revisited* (1984) [2.112].

Research on voting behaviour from the 1950s until the mid-1970s was focused on explaining the stability of Italian voting behaviour. Works published in the 1950s and early 1960s were either methodologically and theoretically weak or experimental and eclectic (the best of them is Alberto Spreafico and Joseph La Palombara, *Elezioni e comportamento politico* (1963) [2.137]), and were based essentially on a class-model of voting behaviour (following work being developed in other west European countries). Research promoted by the Cattaneo Institute in the 1960s (Vittorio Cappechi, V. Cioni Polacchini, Giorgio Galli and Giordano Sivini, *Il comportamento elettorale in Italia* (1968) [2.119]) and also conducted by Samuel Barnes (*Representation in Italy. Institutionalized Tradition and Electoral Choice* (1977) [2.114]) broke with the prevailing view and explained the Italian electorate's stability in terms of deeply rooted sub-cultural traditions of a territorial nature (hence the idea of 'geo-political zones' of which four, North-West, North-East, Centre and South, were identified).

The work funded by the Cattaneo Institute [2.137] was a watershed in electoral studies and influenced all major electoral analysis until the mid-1970s when the 'electoral earthquake' in the national elections of 1976 began to raise questions about the model's continued validity. Research since the mid-1970s has focused on the extent to which the subcultural model has undergone change, with consequent rising levels of electoral volatility. To explain the changes apparently taking place Arturo Parisi and Gianfranco Pasquino, in an influential edited book, *Continuità e mutamento elettorale in Italia* (1977) [2.132] developed a three-fold schema for Italian voting behaviour: *voto d'opinione* (vote of opinion), *voto di scambio* (vote of exchange) and *voto di appartenenza* ('vote of belonging'). They argued that a shift between these types of behaviour was taking place, with a decline in the practice of the third, a diffusion of the second and a widening of the third to a larger number of parties. The simplicity and clarity of this schema, as well as its significance in stressing the importance of the 'qualitative' relationship between voters and parties, resulted in its widespread acceptance and usage. Renato Mannheimer and Giacomo Sani, *Il mercato elettorale. Identikit dell'elettore italiano* (1987) [2.125], in their survey of the political behaviour and attitudes of the Italian electorate in the mid-1980s (based on the results of an opinion poll carried out in 1985) largely confirmed Parisi's and Pasquino's thesis. However, the only work which has specifically attempted to operationalise and test systematically their model (Roberto Cartocci, *Elettori in Italia* (1990) [2.120]) found a persistence in the 'vote of belonging' and a continued weakness in the vote of opinion.

Other work in the 1970s and 1980s has been more specifically focused on the quantitative shifts in Italian voting patterns and the exact meaning of electoral mobility and movement. A landmark in this respect is the work produced by Marzio Barbagli, Piergiorgio Corbetta, Arturo Parisi and Hans M.A. Schadee, *Fluidità elettorale e classi sociali in Italia* (1979) [2.113] which introduced the distinction between individual voting behaviour and aggregate outcome, indicating that increases in individual fluidity should not automatically be assumed to correlate with high levels of aggregate electoral instability (depending on the exact nature of the former and whether different individual shifts effectively cancel each other out in terms of the latter). Their survey of voting behaviour in the 1960s and 1970s found that high levels of individual fluidity in the late 1960s and early 1970s occurred during a period of high aggregate stability. This work (combined with that by Parisi and Pasquino [2.132] published two years earlier) stimulated a considerable amount of research on the meaning and significance of the 'mobility' or 'stability' of the Italian electorate. Important contributions to this debate are: Arturo Parisi (ed), *Mobilità senza movimento* (1980) [2.133]; Renato Mannheimer and Giacomo Sani, *Il mercato elettorale* [2.125]; Renato Mannheimer, *Capire il voto. Contributi per l'analisi del comportamento elettorale delle consultazioni politiche* (1989) [2.126].

In the late 1980s the Cattaneo Institute produced the most comprehensive test of electoral stability. Piergiorgo Corbetta, Arturo Parisi and Hans M.A. Schadee (the authors, less Barbagli, of the 1979 study), *Elezioni in Italia. Struttura e tipologia delle consultazioni politiche* (1988) [2.122] is based on an analysis of aggregate data from the late 1970s onwards, and aimed at assessing electoral volatility (using multiple regression analysis) in the 1970s and 1980s compared with the previous two decades. The authors find no consistent rising trend of electoral instability and reinterpret Italian electoral history in terms of 'electoral cycles' distinguished by three types of elections: mobilization elections (*elezioni di mobilitazione*), demobilization elections (*elezioni di smobilitazione*) and static elections (*elezioni di stallo*).

The dramatic electoral changes of the early 1990s, however, have reignited this debate. The 1992 national elections have received sustained analysis in Patrick McCarthy and Gianfranco Pasquino (eds), *The End of Post-War Politics in Italy. The Landmark 1992 Elections* (1993) [2.128], and in Renato Mannheimer and Giacomo Sani, *La rivoluzione elettorale. L'Italia tra la prima e la seconda repubblica* (1994) [2.127] (which includes an analysis of the important local elections held in 1993). Gianni Statera, *Come votano gli italiani. Dal bipartitismo imperfetto alla crisi del sistema politico* (1993) [2.138] places the 1992 elections in the perspective of electoral change during the 1980s. The 1994 national elections (held under a new electoral system) proved to be an even bigger 'landmark' for psephologists, and are analysed in detail in two excellent books: Stefano Bartolini and Roberto D'Alimonte (eds), *Maggioritario ma non troppo* (1995) [2.115] (originally a special issue of the *Rivista Italiana di Scienza Politica*), and Ilvo Diamanti and Renato Mannheimer (eds), *Milano a Roma. Guida all'Italia elettorale del 1994* (1994) [2.124]. Gabriele Calvi and Andrea Vannucci, *L'Elettore sconosciuto. Analisi socioculturale e segmentazione degli orientamenti politici nel 1994* (1995) [2.118] attempts to establish a link between the social and cultural make-up of Italians and their political choices in 1994, using data gathered by the Eurisko Institute in Spring 1994. From here they are able to argue that, despite the changes in the political parties contesting the 1994 elections, voting behaviour was characterised by considerable stability in terms of the long-term orientations of the electorate.

For those interested in detailed analyses of individual parties Mario Caciagli and Alberto Spreafico (eds), *Vent'anni di elezioni in Italia. 1968-1987* (1990) [2.117] offers the best comparative treatment of all the parties. Bringing together the work of more than a dozen political scientists, the book provides a detailed case study of each political party, followed by analyses of non-voting, the preference vote, referenda and regional and European elections.

As is apparent, research on voting behaviour in Italy has been concentrated on the national level. Detailed empirical analysis of sub-national voting patterns has been rare, with a few exceptions: S. Novelli, *Il voto amministrativo democristiano* (1981) [2.131] attempts to explain why the DC's vote is extremely volatile between elections in some communes while its national vote remains stable; Ilvo Diamanti and Arturo Parisi, *Elezioni a Trieste. Identità territoriale e comportamento di voto* (1991) [2.123] identifies and explains the high degree of electoral volatility in Trieste; AA.VV. *Il comportamento elettorale in Lombardia 1946-1980* (1983) [2.110] provides a comprehensive treatment of electoral behaviour in the postwar period in Lombardy; Part I of Mario Caciagli and Piergiorgio Corbetta (eds), *Elezioni regionali e sistema politico nazionale. Italia, Spagna e Repubblica Federale Tedesca* (1987) [2.116] contains analyses of regional elections and voting behaviour and their relation to politics at the national level.

The debate over changing Italy's electoral system (based on a pure form of proportional representation) grew in intensity during the 1980s and a change to a majoritarian system was eventually achieved, through a combination of a referendum and subsequent parliamentary action, in 1993. The most comprehensive account in English of the historiography of Italian electoral laws is provided in a substantial chapter by Harmut Ullrich in Serge Noiret (ed), *Political Strategies and Electoral Reforms: Origins of Voting Systems in Europe in the 19th. and 20th. Centuries* (1990) [2.130]. The best summary of the most recent debate and of the myriad of proposals for electoral reform made in the last decade is Sebastiano Messina, *La grande riforma* (1993) [2.129] (and the author's preference is made abundantly clear). The course of the debate can also be followed in *Italian Politics: A Review* [2.1] and the contributions to the general debate on institutional reform mentioned in Chapter 3.

Steven Warner and Diego Gambetta, *La retorica della riforma. Fine del sistema proporzionale in Italia* (1994) [2.139] shows the difficulty of achieving specific electoral and political outcomes by changing the electoral system. The book's argument is relevant to electoral systems in all countries. A distinctive and controversial characteristic of the old electoral system was the 'preference vote', where voters could select, in order of preference, up to four candidates. This was regarded as the source of much corruption and was abolished by referendum two years before the electoral system was changed. Pasquale Scaramozzino, *Un'analisi statistica del voto di preferenza in Italia* (1979) [2.136] is one of the few detailed studies of the effects of preference voting. Gianfranco Pasquino (ed), *Votare un solo candidato. Le conseguenze politiche della preferenza unica* (1993) [2.134] brings together various specialists who evaluate the likely impact of the removal of preference voting through an analysis of five case-studies in both 'white' and 'red' regions.

Finally, mention should be made of the referendum which has become increasingly used since the 1970s as a means of achieving reform in the face of an unwilling (or incapable) political class. A useful history of this instrument of direct democracy since the 1970s is provided by Anna Chimenti, *Storia dei Referendum. Dal divorzio alla riforma elettorale* (1993) [2.121]. The book highlights the different types of change that referenda have sought over twenty years, portraying the instrument as an unequivocal positive force. The book was published too early to include an analysis of the important referenda held in 1993 and 1995.

CLIENTELISM AND CORRUPTION

Clientelism has long been identified as a fundamental feature of Italian politics and a significant means by which the governing parties (first the DC, later emulated by others and primarily the PSI) consolidated and maintained their power bases. The most important empirical research on this phenomenon has been carried out at the local level, and specifically on the DC in the South. Percy Allum, *Politics and Society in Post War Naples* (1973) [2.140] is a landmark in this respect. Allum's book is a brilliant analysis of the DC's power base in Naples which uses a refined theoretical framework and is illuminating with respect to the nature of Neapolitan society and its relationship to national politics. Sidney Tarrow, *Peasant Communism in Southern Italy* (1967) [1.56] is also an early and important work in the field. Both books emphasise the importance of massive resource transfers to the South by the central government as an instrument of control by the 'mediating' party, the DC. Their work set the trend for further research in other cities and areas.

Judith Chubb, *Patronage, Power and Poverty in Southern Italy* (1982) [2.148] is a classic analysis of machine politics, which has not been bettered since. Through a case study of Palermo and Naples, the author shows, contrary to the work of some political scientists, that clientelistic political systems do not necessarily need a constantly expanding resource base as a means of maintaining political consent, thanks to local patronage mechanisms which depend only minimally on public resources. Luigi Graziano, *Clientelismo e sistema politico. Il caso dell'Italia* (1979) [2.152], is a study of the DC in Salerno. Mario Caciagli et al., *Democrazia Cristiana e potere nel Mezzogiorno: il sistema democristiano a Catania* (1977) [2.143] analyses the DC in Catania, and, contrary to Chubb, points expressly to the inflationary consequences of clientelism and the need for a constantly expanding resource base. Caroline White, *Patrons and Partisans: A Study of Italian Politics in Two Southern Italian Communities* (1980) [2.159] provides a comparison between political elites and clientele politics in Christian Democratic and Communist-dominated villages in the Abruzzi. James Walston, *The Mafia and Clientelism. Roads to Rome in Post-War Calabria* (1988) [5.146] is a comparison of the relationship between central government and local administration in two cities of Calabria. He attempts to disentangle the relationship between the Mafia and clientelism, evaluating its significance for the distribution of public resources at both the local and national levels.[4]

Work at the national level has been of a slightly different sort. Research has focused primarily on the development of the so-called *parastate* and its subsequent politicisation, but without documenting its clientelistic use in as systematic a way as at the local level (because of the difficulty of carrying out research of this sort at the heart of national government). Books such as Giuseppe Tamburrano, *L'iceberg democristiano* (1974) [2.156], Ruggero Orfei, *L'occupazione del potere: i democristiani '45-'75* (1976) [2.154], Franco Cazzola (ed), *Anatomia del Potere DC - Enti pubblici e 'centralità democristiana'* (1979) [2.146], Giorgio Galli, *L'Italia sotterranea: storia, politica e scandali* (1983) [5.133] document the extraordinary extent to which the main governing party expanded the state and penetrated state agencies. Gabriella Gribaudi, *Mediatori. Antropologia del potere nel Mezzogiorno* (1980) [2.153] looks at the new elites created through the staffing of a whole range of new agencies and boards, often located outside the traditional constitutional framework and unaccountable, therefore, to parliament. Franco Cazzola, *Della Corruzione. Fisiologia e patologia di un sistema politico* (1988) [2.147], provides a broad overview of a hundred years of corruption in Italy, placing corruption under the Republic in useful historical context.

The value of these works is not to be denied. However, the corruption scandals of the late 1980s and early 1990s, which have begun to expose the true extent to which the governing parties' power was based on massive levels of financial corruption in cities of the North as well as the South, and often controlled at the highest national level, suggest that there is still much work to be done on clientelism and political corruption in postwar Italy.

Several books have gone some way to addressing this issue. Donatella Della Porta and Alberto Vannucci, *Corruzione politica e amministrazione pubblica. Risorse, meccanismi, attori* (1994) [2.151], and Marco D'Alberti and Renato Finocchi (eds), *Corruzione e sistema istituzionale* (1994) [2.149] are both impressive works which, in their analyses of political corruption in Italy, show how the subject is a fundamental but as yet understudied aspect of political science and public administration. Vito Marino Caferna, *Il sistema della corruzione. Le ragioni. I soggetti. I luoghi* (1992) [2.144], and Luciano Barca and S. Trento (eds), *L'Economia della corruzione* (1994) [2.142] attempt to unravel the exact mechanics of Italian political corruption. Donatella Della Porta, *Lo scambio politico: Casi di corruzione politica in Italia* (1992) [2.150] considers three instances of corruption involving local governments in the 1980s and is prefaced with a useful theoretical introduction by Alessandro Pizzorno. There are also two books which attempt to locate the scandals of the early 1990s in historical perspective by documenting the development of Italian corruption: Alessandro Silj, *Malpaese. Criminalità, corruzione e politica nell'Italia della prima Repubblica 1943-1994* (1994) [2.155]; and Sergio Turone, *Politica ladra. Storia della corruzione in Italia 1861-1992* (1992) [2.157].

Other useful books (in a field which is now swamped with journalistic accounts) document the scandals and the course of the enquiries, specifically in Milan (where the enquiries began): G. Barbacetto and E. Veltri, *Milan degli scandali* (1991) [2.141] (for the scandals up to 1992), G. Turani and C. Sasso, *I saccheggiatori. Milano: facevano i politici ma erano dei ladri* (1992) [2.158] (on the early months of the judicial enquiries), and A. Carlucci, *Tangentomani. Storie, affari e tutti i documenti sui barbari che hanno saccheggiato Milano* (1992) [2.145] (for a detailed analysis of the most prominent inquests).

NOTES

1. The general works listed here apply also to Chapter 3 on Government.

2. The book was subject to more than one roundtable discussion. For an extensive critical review see Sidney Tarrow, 'Italian Politics and Political Change: "Eppure si muove". But where to?', *West European Politics*, Vol.11, No. 3, 1988, pp. 311-24.

3. It is included here (rather than in the section on social movements in Chapter 5) because it fielded candidates in the 1972 elections.

4. This book is also referred to in the section on the Mafia and the underworld in Chapter 5. Other works cited in that section are obviously relevant here.

3

Government

EXECUTIVE AND LEGISLATURE[1]

There are few full-length political-historical studies of the key formal institutions of Italian government, which is partially a reflection of the failure of these institutions to develop autonomy from the parties. The best general accounts in English are contained in the relevant chapters of David Hine, *Governing Italy* [2.13] and Paul Furlong, *Modern Italy. Representation and Reform* (1994) [3.100]. The best general account in Italian is Giuliano Amato and Augusto Barbera (eds), *Manuale di diritto pubblico* (1984) [3.2], which has separate chapters on each of the key institutions. The best studies of the functioning of the government are: Piero Calandra, *Il Governo della Repubblica* (1986) [3.5]; Sabino Cassese, *Esiste un governo in Italia?* (1980) [3.7]; Sergio Ristucci (ed), *L'istituzione governo: analisi e prospettive* (1977) [3.15]; Luigi Ventura, *Il governo a multipolarità diseguale* (1988) [3.20]; Mauro Calise and Renato Mannheimer, *Governanti in Italia* (1982) [3.6] (the last of which focuses on the elites making up the government).

Literature on the cabinet is primarily legalistic in nature, the two volume work on the cabinet Enrico Spagna Musso (ed), *Costituzione e strutture del governo: il problema della presidenza del Consiglio* (1979-82) [3.18] being typical. Two other useful works are Antonio Ruggeri, *Il Consiglio dei ministri nella costituzione italiana* (1981) [3.16] and Massimo Bonanni (ed), *Governi, ministri, presidenti. Competenze dei ministri, collegialità del governo e funzioni del premier nell'esperienza di tre esecutivi europei: un contributo allo studio del governo in Italia* (1978) [3.4]. Giovanni Pitruzzella, *La presidenza del Consiglio dei ministri e l'organizzazione del governo* (1986) [3.13] provides the most detailed analysis of the Italian Prime Minister and his relations with the cabinet and government. Of a less juridical nature, Roberto Venditti, *Il manuale Cencelli. Il prontuario della lottizzazione democristiana* (1981) [3.19] outlines the informal rules (originally devised by the Christian Democrat Cencelli) which governed the formation of government coalitions during the Christian Democrat era of dominance.

The other institution making up the executive is the presidency which, while primarily ceremonial in nature, can nevertheless have an important influence during crises and the formation of governments. Only one study of significance has been produced on it: A. Baldassare and C. Mezzanotte, *Gli uomini del Quirinale. Da De Nicola a Pertini* (1985) [3.3].

Compared with other legislative bodies, such as the British Parliament and the American Congress, the Italian Parliament is almost unstudied, a reflection of its perceived lack of importance by the academic and political class. Early work by (amongst others) Giovanni Sartori (ed), *Il Parlamento italiano 1946-1963* (1963) [3.17] (which was funded by the Cattaneo Institute), and by Alberto Predieri (ed), *Il parlamento nel sistema politico italiano* (1975) [3.14], failed to promote an interest in the sort of detailed analyses which other legislatures have undergone. For example, there has been no serious work done on important aspects such as the committee system and legislative leadership. The only book length analysis in English is the well-known Giuseppe Di Palma, *Surviving Without Governing: the Italian Parties in Parliament* (1977) [3.9] which concluded that the Italian parliament was in crisis as a result of its failure to have obtained the legitimacy experienced by most other legislatures. A more up to date text, which argues for the increased centrality of parliament in the institutional system, is the second edition of Andrea Manzella, *Il Parlamento* (1991) [3.11], which also provides the most detailed guide to the institution's rules and recent rule changes. Some empirical work has been done on the legislators themselves and their routes to office, of which Maurizio Cotta, *Classe politica e parlamento in Italia* (1979) [3.8] is particularly noteworthy.

The two other sources of information on the functioning of key institutions are firstly, the volumes of *Italian Politics: A Review* [2.1], and secondly the debate on institutional reform. This debate has produced a wealth of literature which is all in Italian because most of it is written by the protagonists themselves. Nonetheless, some of the texts display a keen awareness of the working and malfunctioning of the key Italian institutions, even if many of them have been surpassed by the reforms which have been achieved. Particularly noteworthy in this respect are Giuliano Amato, *Una Repubblica da riformare* (1980) [3.1] and Gianfranco Pasquino, *Restituire lo scettro al principe. Proposte di riforma istituzionale* (1985) [3.12]. Carlo Fusaro, *Guida alle riforme istituzionale. Per capire le proposte di cui si parla* (1992) [3.10] provides a more up to date guide to the debate, although even this has been overtaken by the reforms achieved in the early 1990s.

JUDICIARY AND LEGAL SYSTEM

The judiciary has been largely neglected by political scientists and monopolised by Italian jurists, with the result that much of the work is legalistic in nature. Nonetheless, there are several works which stand out. The best analysis of the structure and power of the judiciary and its relationship with other institutions of the state is Alessandro Pizzorusso, *L'organizzazione della giustizia in Italia. La magistratura nel sistema politico e istituzionale* (1982) [3.29]. A more general overview is provided by Romano Canosa and Pietro Federico, *La magistratura in Italia dal 1945 a oggi* (1974) [3.21]. Stefano Rodotà, *La corte costituzionale* (1986) [3.30] is probably the best account of the structures and power of the Constitutional Court. Giorgio Freddi, *Tensioni e conflitto nella magistratura. Un'analisi istituzionale dal dopoguerra al 1968* (1977) [3.25] is a useful analysis of the internal politics of the judiciary, and Sergio Pappalardo, *Gli iconoclasti. Magistratura democratica nel quadro della associazione nazionale magistrati* (1987) [3.28] is an analysis of the left-wing faction of the judiciary which emerged in the 1970s, the so-called democratic magistrates. Carlo Guarnieri, *L'indipendenza della magistratura* (1981) [3.26] assesses the degree of autonomy enjoyed by the judiciary.

A social scientific (as opposed to legalistic) approach was spurred on by the revival of interest in the judiciary in the late 1980s and 1990s. In this context, two books should be noted: Carlo Guarnieri, *Magistratura e politica in Italia* (1993) [3.27]; and F. Zannotti, *La magistratura. Un gruppo di pressione istituzionale* (1989) [3.31]. The emergence of the judiciary as a significant factor in exposing political corruption in the early 1990s and the ensuing conflict with parties and politicians has stimulated a new agenda for research which should result in new social scientific research on a still understudied institution.

The most extensive general treatment of the Italian legal system in English is G. L. Certoma, *The Italian Legal System* (1985) [3.23] (which effectively replaces the good but now dated text produced by Mauro Cappelletti et al., *The Italian Legal System* (1967) [3.22]). There is, as yet, no full length account of the new code of criminal procedure which was introduced in 1989. Finally, a useful guide to Italian law and the legal system is provided by the *Enciclopedia del Diritto* [3.24].

SUB-NATIONAL GOVERNMENT AND CENTRE-PERIPHERY RELATIONS

The study of centre-periphery relations and sub-national governments was long dominated by a legalistic approach, with the result that most of the literature was written from an institutional and historical perspective, with little empirically based research. However, in the past decade or so this dominance has been partially eroded by new studies in political science.

The most comprehensive guide to centre-periphery relations is the three volume work by the ISAP (Istituto per la scienza dell'amministrazione pubblica), *Le relazioni centro-periferia* (1984) [3.38]. The three volumes contain over fifty articles, the first two volumes being devoted to Italy, and the third volume to other countries. Although the legalistic tradition is apparent in these volumes (through the emphasis of many articles on legal structures and legally-defined powers), these are integrated with a series of empirical articles more characteristic of advanced social science. The breadth of themes is particularly praiseworthy with, for example, the inclusion of political parties, trade unions, employers' organisations and the judiciary.

The best analysis of centre-periphery relations in a single volume is Bruno Dente, *Governare la frammentazione. Stato, regioni ed enti locali in Italia* (1985) [3.35]. For English readers, the best treatments pre-date the full functioning of regional governments in Italy, but this is not to take away their importance. Robert Fried, *The Italian Prefect* (1963) [3.36] is a good analysis of the workings of centre-periphery relations in the 1950s and 1960s, through its focus on the role of the Prefect. Sidney Tarrow, *Between Center and Periphery. Grassroots Politicians in Italy and France* (1977) [3.45], is an impressive piece of research in comparative politics which highlights the importance of political parties and informal channels of communication between centre and periphery in Italy (as opposed to the formal bureaucratic structures of such importance in France).

The implementation of regional governments in 1970 after 22 years of procrastination by successive Italian governments has generated some important research by foreign scholars, some of which has already been noted above. As with centre-periphery relations, the most comprehensive survey is provided by the ISAP in a two volume study, *La regionalizzazione* 1983) [3.37], which documents the progress and nature of regional autonomy both in Italy and some other democracies. Perhaps the most innovative research has been completed by Robert Putnam, Robert Leonardi and Raffaella Nanetti in *La pianta e le radici. Il radicamento dell'istituto regionale nel sistema politico italiano* (1985) [3.44] (and which provided the basis for *Making Democracy Work* [2.20]). Based on data collected since the introduction of the regional system, this book investigates the progress of, and reasons behind, the institutionalisation of the regional governments in the Italian political system, thus providing valuable insights for comparative politics and the analysis of new institutions in any political system. One of the major conclusions of this work is that the historical and social/contexts in which the regional governments operate are significant explanatory factors in how well they perform from the perspective of administration and policy-making.

The authors also developed their findings and extended their data to provide more sustained analyses of individual regions: Robert Leonardi, Robert Putnam and Raffaella Nanetti, *Il caso Basilicata: l'effetto regione dal 1970 al 1986* (1987) [3.39], and Robert Leonardi and Raffaella Nanetti (eds), *The Regions and European Integration. The Case of Emilia-Romagna* (1991) [3.40]. This last volume's analysis by a group of specialists of the region's political developments, institutions, economic performance, policy-making and culture in the context of its ties with other regions and the European Community provides an essential means of understanding the so-called 'Emilian model' of development (see Chapter 4).

A comprehensive analysis of local government is made by Franco Cazzola, *Perifici integrati. Chi, dove, quando nelle amministrazioni comunali* (1991) [3.34]. Of similar quality is the two volume study on local government functions: Francesco Merloni, Vincenzo Santatonio and Luisa Torchia, *Le funzioni del governo locale in Italia. Vol. 1. Il dato normativo* (1988) [3.41], and S. Mannozzi and V. Visco Comandini, *Le funzioni del governo locale in Italia. Vol 2. Verifica dell'effettività* (1990) [3.42]. A useful empirical analysis of local finance is provided in Giovanni Maltinti and Alessandro Petretto (eds), *Finanziamento ed efficenza della spesa pubblica locale* (1987) [3.43], and the role and performance of local councillors is evaluated in Gianfranco Bettin and Annick Magnier, *Chi governa la città? Una ricerca sugli assessori comunali* (1991) [3.33]. Finally, a useful annual reference work for those researching local government is the *Annuario delle autonomie locali* (1981-) [3.32].

ADMINISTRATION AND CIVIL SERVICE

Studying the main institutions which make up the national administrative system -- the bureaucracy, the special agencies, the army and the police -- has not proved popular amongst Italians or foreigners, and particularly the latter. There are no full length studies of the Italian state bureaucracy in English beyond the general politics texts listed in the first section of Chapter 2, and beyond the general context of the Christian Democratic party (Chapter 2, section on parties: individual studies). The best research carried out in Italian (see also the section on public bodies below) is that associated with Sabino Cassese. His *Il sistema amministrativo italiano* (1983) [3.51] and an earlier edited collection, *L'amministrazione pubblica in Italia* (1974) [3.49] are excellent accounts of the nature, development and malfunctioning of the bureaucracy and so-called *parastate* (which will be touched on more fully in the section on policy-making below). *Le basi del diritto amministrativo* (1989) [3.53], by the same author, is a more general work, but Italy constitutes the main focus of its examination of the origins of administrative rules and law. The other key general text on the Italian public administration is Massimo Severo Giannini, *Istituzioni di diritto amministrativo* (1982) [3.63].

The best work (although primarily legalistic in orientation) on the structure of government and ministries is Enrico Spagna Musso (ed), *Costituzione e struttura del governo: la riforma dei ministri* (1984) [3.70]. A useful statistical compendium of the administration is provided by the Istituto Centrale di Statistica, *Statistiche sulla amministrazione pubblica* (1991) [3.65]. The relationship between the bureaucracy and politicians is explored in Franco Ferraresi, *Burocrazia e politica in Italia* (1980) [3.62]. The poor performance of the Italian bureaucracy is evaluated in G. Pennella (ed), *La produttività nella pubblica amministrazione: rapporto al Consiglio nazionale dell'economia e del lavoro* (1987) [3.67]. A less thorough study of its performance but a more enjoyable read is Gianfranco Bianchi, *L'Italia dei ministeri: lo sfascio guidato* (1981) [3.47]. The work of Roberto Ruffilli on public administration should also be mentioned. Although his most significant work was on the pre-war period, his writings cover a vast trajectory of Italian institutional and bureaucratic history. His complete writings have been gathered together in three volumes, *Istituzioni, Società, Stato* (1989-91) [3.68]. Writings on the public and semi-public agencies are analysed in the section on policy making in this chapter and in Chapter 4 below. A basic guide to all public institutions is Sergio Travaglio (ed), *Come funziona l'Italia* (1994) [3.71]. Arranged alphabetically, it covers all the main public, semi-public and private institutions, accompanied by graphs, tables and statistics.

There has been little empirical work on the attitudes of Italian civil servants since Putnam's comparative study of senior civil servants in the early 1970s, which is contained in Mattei Dogan (ed), *The Mandarins of Western Europe* (1975) [3.61]. Nonetheless, some Italian works on the bureaucracy are useful in this respect. Three general works on public sector employment are: M. Rusciani, *L'impiego pubblico in Italia* (1978) [3.69]; G. Cercora (ed), *Il pubblico impiego: struttura e retribuzioni* (1991) [3.54]; and Marco D'Alberti (ed), *La dirigenza pubblica* (1990) [3.58]. Sabino Cassesse (ed), *L'amministrazione centrale* (1984) [3.52] is a useful collection which reveals the legalistic and obstructionist tendencies of the civil service. His *Questione amministrativa e questione meridionale. Dimensioni e reclutamento della burocrazia dall'Unità ad oggi* (1977) [3.50] outlines the 'southernisation' of the state bureaucracy and its accompanying effects. Finally, Ermano Gorrieri, *La giungla retributiva* ('the remuneration jungle') (1972) [3.64] has entered Italian academic parlance in its vivid description of the myriad laws and regulations governing pay and conditions in the Civil Service.

The only notable books on the police are Romano Canosa, *La polizia in Italia dal 1945 ad oggi* (1976) [3.48], and Angelo D'Orsi, *Il potere repressivo. La polizia. Le forze dell'ordine italiano* (1972) [3.59]. The role of the army has been similarly neglected. Indeed, contemporary Italianists have rarely shown an interest in the important relationship between military and police institutions and civilian authority, apart from when they are protagonists in scandals such as the planned *coup* of 1964 (on which see R. Collin, *The De Lorenzo Gambit: the Italian Coup Manqué of 1964* (1977) [3.57]). An exception in English is J. Whittam, *The Politics of the Italian Army* (1977) [3.72]. Enea Cerquetti, *Le forze armate dal 1945 al 1975. Strutture e dottrine* (1975) [3.55] is the best account of how the postwar development of the armed forces was shaped and influenced by the Cold War and the assistance of the United States. Also useful is AA.VV, *Il potere militare in Italia* (1971) [3.46]. Lucio Ceva, *Le forze armate* (1981) [3.56] contains only a short epilogue on the postwar period, but is nevertheless useful for historical context.

More interest of late has been shown in the security services, mainly because of their expected collusion in right wing terrorist outrages. Indeed, recent revelations show that knowledge about the security services is essential to understanding Italy's instabilities in the postwar period. Despite the evident difficulties of carrying out research in this area, a good history is provided by Giuseppe De Lutiis, *Storia dei servizi segreti in Italia* (1984) [3.60]. More impressive is Claudio Gatti, *Rimanga tra noi. L'America, l'Italia, la "questione comunista": i segreti di 50 anni di storia* (1990) [5.135], although this is not a straightforward history of the secret services, but rather a detailed account of the role of the United States in the more obscure events and happenings of the Italian Republic, based on a wealth of American archive material. The English equivalent (although not in terms of academic quality) is Philip Willan, *Puppet Masters. The Political Use of Terrorism in Italy* [5.147]. Despite its journalistic style, the book provides a good analysis of the Italian and American security services' role in planned *coups* and terrorism of the right and manipulation of terrorism of the left. For non-Italian readers it is the only book in English to document the murkier side of the role of the

Italian and American secret services in the development of the postwar republic, including the establishment of the secret anti-communist military organisation, *Gladio*.

Finally, although Italy is a republic, mention should be made of the monarchy. Its historical influence, the fact that it was abolished by a very narrow majority and that there existed a monarchist party in the postwar period suggests that an historical understanding of this institution should not be neglected. Dennis Mack Smith's *Italy and its Monarchy* (1989) [3.66] is a splendid account.

PUBLIC AND SEMI-PUBLIC BODIES

Postwar Italy has had a unique system of public intervention based on special agencies such as the Institute for Industrial Reconstruction (IRI). These agencies have exercised a considerable degree of autonomy from government authority and, controlling a large number of companies themselves, have been given a national role in assisting investment and growth in industry. A knowledge of the complexities of the so-called 'IRI model' of public intervention is essential to understanding the international success of Italian state-controlled industry in the immediate postwar period and Italy's 'economic miracle'. It is also essential to understanding how the special agencies (not just in the economic sector but also in the social services sector) were used by the governing parties to reinforce their hold on power and how the formula subsequently entered into crisis. There are two books in English which, despite their age, are still essential for understanding this mode of state intervention in the economy: M. V. Posner and Stuart J. Woolf, *Italian Public Enterprise* (1967) [3.77], and Stuart Holland (ed), *The State as Entrepreneur. New Dimensions for Public Enterprise: the IRI State-Holding Formula* (1972) [3.74].

Later works, which also provide broader overviews of all the special agencies and their political use, include: Pasquale Saraceno, *Il sistema delle imprese a partecipazione statale* (1975) [3.78]; G. Maggia and Graziella Fornengo, *Appunti sul sistema delle partecipazioni statali* (1976) [3.75]; Donatello Serrani, *Il potere per enti: Enti pubblici e sistema politico in Italia* (1978) [3.79]; E. Gerelli and G. Boghetti (eds), *La crisi delle partecipazioni statali: motivi e prospettivi* (1981) [3.73]. The most exhaustive historical study of public and semi-public agencies is *Gli enti pubblici italiani: anagrafe legislative e giurisprudenziali dal 1861 al 1970* (1972) [3.76], which is introduced by Alberto Mortara and is part of the Ciriec book series. There is as yet no single text which has documented the unprecedented changes the Italian public sector model has been (falteringly) undergoing since privatisation was begun in the mid-1980s, but they have been partially analysed in the pages of *Italian Politics: A Review* [2.1]. Further works in this general area may be found in Chapter 4.

PUBLIC POLICIES AND DOMESTIC POLICY-MAKING

Public policies and policy-making in Italy have not received the degree of attention typical of other major European countries. This, as Maurizio Ferrera has argued, is primarily due to the fact that when, in the early 1960s, the issue of state intervention and policy-making became a major issue, Italian political science had not taken off as a discipline, and was therefore in no position to analyse it.[2] This was in stark contrast to countries such as the United States, where political science was sufficiently mature to deal with public policies. Consequently, Italian public policy became the preserve of academics with a legal, economic and sociological background. The influence of political scientists was marginal until the early 1980s (although it was growing in the 1970s) and policy analysis still represents only a small part of Italian political science today. The best overall analysis of public policy is Bruno Dente (ed), *Le politiche pubbliche in Italia* (1990) [3.90], which is divided into four parts covering institutional policies, economic policies, land policies and social policies. Important work has been carried out on the process of policy formation and implementation by Bruno Dente (ed), *Politiche pubbliche e pubblica amministrazione* (1989) [3.91] and M. Morisi, *Parlamento e politiche pubbliche* (1988) [3.107]. In English, Peter Lange and Marino Regini (eds), *State, Market and Social Regulation: New Perspectives on Italy* (1989) [4.69] is a first-rate book dealing with the regulation of the economy, industrial relations and the welfare state. A good introduction in English to public policy-making in Italy is Paul Furlong, *Modern Italy. Representation and Reform* (1994) [3.100], which also adopts a comparative framework in order to show the similarities and differences between Italy and its European neighbours. Mention should also be made of Giuliano Amato, *Economia, politica, istituzioni* (1976) [3.81], which was one of the first significant attempts at providing an overall interpretation of Italian public policy-making, based on the idea of a 'spoils-distributing' government (*governo spartitorio*). Although the interpretation was modified by later research, the essential thrust of the work is still relevant. Amato's book, in fact, was a more general development of his seminal work *Il governo dell'industria in Italia* (1971) [3.80], which explored the relationship between the industrial and political systems and helped promote extensive research on the bureaucracy and the DC (already cited in the section on the DC above and in Chapter 2).

If a single event can be identified which prompted more systematic research into public policy-making it was the birth of the Italian welfare state in 1978. This watershed in the social history of postwar Italy is admirably analysed in two volumes both of which emphasise the politicisation and clientelism prevalent in the system: Ugo Ascoli (ed), *Welfare state all'italiana* (1984) [3.86], and Maurizio Ferrera, *Il Welfare state in Italia: Sviluppo e crisi in prospettiva comparata* (1984) [3.94]. A synthesis of the latter work in English appears in Volume 2 of Peter Flora (ed), *Growth to Limits: the West European Welfare States since World War II* (1986) [3.97]. A more recent analysis which takes account of important changes after 1992 is provided by Giuliano Cazzola, *Lo stato sociale tra crisi e riforme: il caso Italia* (1994) [3.88]. Achille Ardigò and F. Barbano (eds), *Medici e sociosanitari: professioni in transizione* (1981) [3.84] and Achille Ardigò, *Per una rifondazione del welfare state* (1985) [3.85] evaluate the crisis of the welfare state, the latter with a heavy prescriptive element.

Two books which adopt a comparative perspective to analyse the organisational impact of the changes in the Italian national health service since 1978 are Maurizio Ferrera and Giovanna Zincone (eds), *Le salute che noi pensiamo: domande sanitari e politiche pubbliche in Italia* (1986) [3.96], and Giorgio Freddi (ed), *Rapporto Perkoff* (1984) [3.98]. Maurizio Ferrera, *Modelli di solidarità: politica e riforme sociali nelle democrazie* (1993) [3.95] is a comparative text which attempts to explain the differences in the number and type of people covered by welfare benefits. The book contains a specific section devoted to the Italian case and is essential reading to understand Italy's form of distinctive development.

The history of the Italian social security system until 1960 is told by Arnaldo Cherubini, *Storia della previdenza sociale in Italia (1860-1960)* (1977) [3.89], and its organisational and financial structure is analysed by Domenicantonio Fausto, *Il sistema italiano di sicurezza sociale* (1978) [3.93]. The specific complexities and arbitrariness of the Italian pensions system are admirably unravelled by Onorato Castellino, *Il labrinto delle pensioni* (1976) [3.87].

The Italian school system is analysed in an excellent work by Anna Laura Fadiga Zanatta, *Il sistema scolastico italiano* (1971) [3.92], and educational policies more generally are evaluated by L. Livolsi et al., *La macchina del vuoto* (1974) [3.105] and Fiorella Padoa Schioppa, *Scuola e classi sociali* (1974) [3.108]. Postwar housing policy and town planning is covered in A. Fubini, *Urbanistica in Italia* (1976) [3.99] and G. Rochat, G. Sateriale and L. Spano, *La casa in Italia, 1945-1980. Alle radici del potere democristiano* (1980) [3.106].

Italian environmentalism appears to be still in its early stages despite rising levels of pollution and several ecological disasters in the late 1980s and this is reflected in the paucity of literature. Apart from statistical accounts (and the best of these is the two volume set by ISTAT, *Statistiche ambientali* (1984) [3.102]), the most comprehensives accounts of the environment and its pollution are: Giorgio Amendola, P.G. Cannata, L. Conti, P. Degli, F.Espinasa, F. Giovenale, F. Karrer, M. Libertini, G. Nebbia, G. Pinchera, E. Reallici, *Il malpaese: rapporto sull'ambiente* (1983) [3.83]; U. Leone, *Geografia per l'ambiente* (1987) [3.103]; Giorgio Amendola and C. Botré, *Italia inquinata* (1978) [3.82]. Government action in the environmental arena, and the problematic emergence of a proper environmental policy (urged by changing public attitudes and the development of an environment policy by the European Union, but hampered by the compartmentalised and fragmented nature of the Italian system of government), is the subject of N. Greco, *La valutazione di impatto ambientale: rivoluzione o compilazione amministrativa?* (1984) [3.101] . Probably the best case study of policy-making in this area is R. Lewansky's analysis of water pollution, *Il controllo degli inquinamenti delle acque: l'attuazione di una politica pubblica* (1986) [3.104].

FOREIGN POLICY AND EUROPEAN INTEGRATION

Apart from relations between Italy and the United States in the postwar reconstruction period, Italy's foreign policy and foreign relations have not been a popular area of study, something which is a reflection of a largely inactive foreign policy and one which has been viewed as essentially servile to the interests of the United States. Academic attention to this area has begun to change as a result both of Italy becoming more active on the international scene and of the accelerated pace of European integration.

Early works include: Massimo Bonnani (ed), *La politica estera della repubblica italiana* (1967) [3.110]; Luigi Graziano, *La politica estera italiana nel dopoguerra* (1968) [3.116]; Primo Vannicelli, *Italy, NATO and the European Community* (1974) [3.125]; and, on the influences at work in the making of foreign policy, Norman Kogan, *The Politics of Italian Foreign Policy* (1963) [3.119]. The most comprehensive work until the end of the 1970s was that carried out under the auspices of the Istituto Affari Internazionali: Natalino Ronzitti (ed), *La Politica Estera Italiana. Autonomia, interdipendenza, integrazione e sicurezza* (1977) [3.123].

The two best recent accounts of foreign policy are the edited collection by Richard Bosworth and Sergio Romano, *La Politica Estera Italiana: 1860-1985* (1991) [3.111], which charts the continuities in foreign policy from Unification to the 1980s, and Carlo Santoro, *La politica estera di una media potenza. L'Italia dall'Unità ad oggi* (1991) [3.124]. The latter work, besides providing an historical overview, also has a good analysis of the key actors making up the foreign policy 'community', and is an important contribution to this area of study.

There is no single volume which addresses Italian security policy. It has been analysed generally in the context of southern European security as a whole, on which there are two useful books: Roberto Aliboni (ed), *Southern European Security in the*

1990s (1992) [3.109] (especially the chapter by Greco and Guazzone); and John Chipman (ed), *NATO's Southern Allies: Internal and External Challenges* (1988) [3.112] (especially the chapter by Cremasco). A useful general yearbook published by the Istituto Affari Internazionali is *L'Italia nella politica internazionale* [3.117].

Specific coverage of European integration has been no more comprehensive. Italy has suffered from being, in a certain sense, an odd man out, despite being a founder member of the European Economic Community (EEC). On the one hand, the country has never been regarded as significant an actor in the European Community (EC) and, later, European Union (EU), as Germany, France and Britain. On the other hand, Italy did not receive the degree of attention and analysis enjoyed by other southern European countries (Spain, Portugal and Greece) when they joined the EC in the early 1980s. This lack of attention has been partially rectified by a comparative research project on the development of the European Union and the member states, although the historical sweep of this work has thus far only reached 1952. In particular, the work of Simona Colarizzi and Saverio Galante on parties and interest groups is to be recommended in Ennio di Nolfo (ed), *Power in Europe? II Great Britain, France, Germany and Italy and the Origins of the EEC, 1952-1957* (1992) [3.113].

The European policy of Alcide De Gasperi, the first Prime Minister of the Republic and the man most responsible for shaping Italy's international outlook in the immediate postwar period, is contained in G. Petrilli, *La politica estera ed europea di De Gasperi* (1975) [3.121]. Good documentary material on parties and pressure groups is to be found in the chapter by Sergio Pistone in Walter Lipgens and Wilfred Loth (eds), *Documents on the History of European Integration. Volume 3: The Struggle for European Union by Political Parties and Interest Groups in Western European Countries 1945-1950* (1988) [3.120]. A general account of the different party positions until the mid-1970s towards Europe and the emergence of a consensus on the issue is provided by Richard Walker, *Dal confronto al consenso. I partiti politici italiani e l'integrazione europea* (1976) [3.126]. The specific shift in position of the Italian Communist Party (PCI), which created the bedrock of the consensus, is charted in Saverio Galante, *Il Partito comunista italiano e l'integrazione europea* (1988) [3.115].

More general sources include: *L'Italia e Europa* [3.118], which is a yearbook; Sergio Pistone (ed), *L'Italia e L'Unità Europea. Dalle premesse storiche all'elezione del Parlamento europeo* (1982) [3.122], which is a collection of key documents; Roy F. Willis, *Italy Chooses Europe* (1971) [3.127], which is a largely descriptive historical account of Italy's approach to European integration until 1970. The best English-language introduction to Italy and the European Union in the contemporary context is Francesco Francioni (ed), *Italy and EC Membership Evaluated* (1992) [3.114]. Part of a series of texts on the member states published by Pinter, the book brings together the work of a dozen specialists who analyse the various economic and social policies relevant to the EC, Italy's foreign relations and the impact of the EC on the Italian political and legal systems. The emphasis is on a cost-benefit analysis of Italy's membership, which makes parts of the book not so suitable for the beginner.

NOTES

1. For general works on government see the first section of Chapter 2. For works on the Constitution see the section on the post war settlement, Chapter 1.

2. Maurizio Ferrera, 'Italian political science and public policies. A late but promising encounter', *European Journal of Political Research*, 21, 1992. Parts of this section draw on Ferrera's excellent analysis.

4

Economy

GENERAL WORKS

The best introductory work available on the Italian economy in English is (despite its age) Kevin J. Allen and A. A. Stevenson, *An Introduction to the Italian Economy* (1975) [4.1]. It summarises in a clear and accessible style for non-economists the basic characteristics and dualistic development of the Italian economy as well as providing a good bibliography for those wishing to study the subject further. Donald Templeman, *The Italian Economy* (1981) [4.16] is also a useful introduction. Good introductory histories of the postwar economy are provided by: Gisele Podbielski, *Italy: Development and Crisis in the Postwar Economy* (1974) [4.14]; Augusto Graziani (ed), *L'economia italiana: 1945-1970* (1971) [4.9]; and the first part of Donald Sassoon, *Contemporary Italy* [2.21].

None of these accounts is recent enough to analyze the changes of the 1980s and the current economy. Three good texts cover this most recent period. Of these the most accessible is the first-rate work by Fiorella Padoa Schioppa, *Italy. The Sheltered Economy* (1993) [4.12], which is an astute analysis of Italy's economic problems. Carluccio Bianchi and Carlo Casarosa (eds), *The Recent Performance of the Italian Economy. Market Outcomes and State Policy* (1991) [4.3] is the product of an international conference held in 1989 at the University of Pisa. The book includes analyses (some of which are rather specialist for the general reader) of macroeconomic policy, balance of payments constraints, trade performance, industrial strategies, economic development, the labour market and exchange rate and common market policies. Adolfo Battaglia and Roberto Valcamonici (eds), *Nella competizione globale. Una politica industriale verso il 2000* (1990) [4.4] is the outcome of research conducted for the Italian Ministry of Industry in 1988-89 by specialists from government, public agencies and the universities. The book focuses on Italy's place in the world economy and its prospects for economic integration into the European Union in the light of its many economic problems.

The best regular reports on the Italian economy are produced by the Bank of Italy (*Banco d'Italia* [4.2]), *Confindustria* [4.5] (the main employers' association), the *Organisation for Economic Cooperation and Development* (OECD) [4.11], the *Economist Intelligence Unit* (EIU) [4.7] and those contained in the regular surveys in the *Financial Times* [4.8] and the *Economist* [4.6]. The *Review of the Economic Conditions in Italy* [4.15] and *Journal of Regional Policy* [4.10] (a translation of *Mezzogiorno d'Europa*) are also good resources (the latter includes the annual report of the Governor of the Bank of Italy). Finally, students interested in the work of Italian economists will find L. Pasinetti (ed), *Italian Economic Papers* (1992-) [4.13] indispensable. This is a series of volumes which translates the best work of Italian economists, past and present.

ECONOMIC DEVELOPMENT

There is a long tradition of studying Italy's economic development and agricultural, industrial and business structure. The decline in the importance of agriculture in the postwar period is charted in Camillo Daneo, *Breve storia dell'agricoltura italiana* (1980) [4.30], while Russell King analyses one of the few major reforms of the 1950s in *Land Reform: the Italian Experience* (1980) [4.41]. Useful overviews of Italian industrial development are provided by R. Romeo, *Breve storia della grande industria in Italia* (1972) [4.52], and Valerio Castronovo, *L'industria italiana dall'Ottocento a oggi* (1980) [4.29]. A useful introductory analysis of Italian industry from a geographic context is provided by Russell King, *The Industrial Geography of Italy* (1985) [4.42]. The internationalisation of Italian industry is the subject of Fabrizio Onida and Gianfranco Viesti (eds), *The Italian Multinationals* (1988) [4.46]. It analyses the size, geographical and sectoral distribution and strategic position of Italian multinationals, explaining how and why they internationalised themselves and what they gained from it.

The dominant theme in studies of the economy has been (and, to a large extent, remains) that of Italy's 'dualism', which has three closely interrelated contrasts: first, between one part of the economy which is technologically advanced with high levels of productivity and a more traditional part of the economy which is more labour intensive and with low levels of productivity; second, between part of the economy comprising very large firms and part comprising thousands of very small firms, with the absence of much medium-sized enterprise in between; third, between a rapidly developing North and a backward and under developed South. The classic study of Italian dualism in English is Vera Lutz, *Italy: a Study in Development* (1962) [4.43], which develops a theoretical framework to study dualistic development and then applies it to the North-South divide in Italy. Also worthy of mention is George H. Hildebrand, *Growth and Structure in the Economy of Modern Italy* (1965) [4.38] which, in its emphasis on the importance of small firms to the Italian economy, was a precursor of what would become a significant debate in the 1970s and 1980s. Vittorio Valli, *L'economia e la politica economica italiana 1945-1975* (1977) [4.58] is also a useful work. A more sophisticated and up-to-date analysis of dualism is to be found in the comparative work of Suzanne Berger and Michael Piore, *Dualism and Discontinuity in Industrial Societies* (1980) [4.21].

Of the three aspects of Italy's dualism, the territorial divide (between North and South) was for a long time the main focus of academic study. Indeed, *la questione meridionale* (the 'Southern Question') has been studied since the beginning of the century, and has generated a vast literature spanning various disciplines (as is apparent from works cited in other chapters) because the problem has not been perceived in purely economic terms. Sidney Sonnino, Giustino Fortunato, Gaetano Salvemini, Guido Dorso and Antonio Gramsci are some of the famous Italian authors and protagonists who have focused much of their writing on the Southern Question. The best anthology of this work is provided by Rosario Villari (ed), *Il Sud nella storia d'Italia: antologia della questione meridionale* (1974) [4.59]. The most comprehensive analysis of the Southern Question, linking its economic, social and political elements, is Carlo Triglia, *Sviluppo senza autonomia* (1992) [4.57], although Carlo Donolo et al., *Classi sociali e politica nel Mezzogiorno: materiali per l'analisi della società meridionale* (1978) [4.31] is also an excellent analysis of the South's distinctive social and political structures. Other useful works focusing on detailed economic aspects include: Sandro Petriccioni, *Politica industriale e Mezzogiorno* (1976) [4.47]; Augusto Graziani and E. Pugliese (eds), *Investimenti e disoccupazione nel Mezzogiorno* (1979) [4.37]; N. Boccella, *Il Mezzogiorno sussidiato: reddito prodotto e trasferimenti alle famiglie nei comuni meridionali* (1982) [4.25]; Eyvind Hytten and Marco Marchioni, *Industrializzazione senza sviluppo. Gela: una storia meridionale* (1970) [4.40], which is a case study of Gela showing the impact of setting up large corporations in a backward economy: 'industrialisation without development'. In English (besides the general texts cited in the first section of this chapter) the best treatments are Alan B. Mountjoy, *The Mezzogiorno* (1973) [4.44], and Kevin Allen and M. C. MacLennan, *Regional Problems and Policies in Italy and France* (1970) [4.17].

The 1980s and 1990s saw the emergence of a 'revisionist' approach to the 'Southern Question' among historians such as Giuseppe Giarrizzo, Gabriella Gribaudi, Maria Petrusewicz and Piero Bevilacqua. They argue that the Southern Question is, to a large extent, artificial. Its origins can be traced to the politics of the late nineteenth century rather than economic reality and its continued existence is maintained largely by comparing the South to a level of development 'normally' expected in advanced European democracies. Consequently, all research into the South has been distorted because it has started from these premises. The revisionists' quest is to analyse the 'South without meridionalisation', the title of a book by Giuseppe Giarrizzo which is the best example of the revisionist approach: *Mezzogiorno senza meridionalismo. La Sicilia, lo sviluppo, il potere* (1992) [4.33]. Paolo Pezzino, *Il paradiso abitato dai diavoli. Società, élites, istituzioni nel Mezzogiorno contemporaneo* (1992) [4.48] is an interesting collection of articles which, taking into account the revisionist approach but not embracing it unequivocally, looks at centre-periphery relations from the perspective of the modernisation of the South. For a vivid (journalistic) picture of conditions in the south in the 1990s Giorgio Bocca, *L'inferno. Profondo sud, male oscuro* (1992) [4.24] is to be recommended.

Accounts of Italian postwar economic development produced in the 1960s tended to be infused with optimism because of the economic miracle the country was undergoing and how this appeared to fit in with the then prevalent 'modernisation' theories (under which problems such as dualism would disappear). Typical examples of this trend (besides the works cited by Hildebrand [4.38] and Lutz [4.43] above), were Pasquale Saraceno (a leading Christian Democrat economist), *L'Italia verso la piena occupazione* (1963) [4.54], and M.R. Stern, *Foreign Trade and Growth in Italy* (1967) [4.55]. Stern's book is the best account in English of Italy's export-led model of growth in this decade, matched in Italian by Augusto Graziani et al., *Lo sviluppo di una economia aperta* (1969) [4.35]. The economic, social and political problems of the 1970s shattered this false optimism and led to a more crisis-infused literature epitomised in Augusto Graziani (ed), *Crisi e ristrutturazione dell'economia italiana* (1975) [4.36], Michele Salvati, *Il sistema economico italiano: analisi di una crisi* (1975) [4.53], and in more general collections edited by Luigi Graziano and Sidney Tarrow, *La crisi italiana* [1.73], and F.L. Cavazza and Stephen R. Graubard, *Il caso italiano* [1.67].

This literature, in turn, was modified by the publication of Arnaldo Bagnasco, *Tre Italie: la problematica territoriale dello sviluppo italiano* (1977) [4.18], which marked a fundamental turning point in the study of Italian dualism and the political economy. Bagnasco's thesis is that there was, in the 1950s and 1960s, a pattern of differentiated economic growth which had effectively created 'Three Italies' with different industrial structures and business cultures, rather than the two traditionally associated with the North-South divide: a Northwestern area characterised by older, heavy industry and large-scale factory production; a Central and Northeastern area of small family-based firms producing goods for export to customised rather than mass markets; and the South which remained underdeveloped and dependent on government subsidies and employment. Bagnasco's book is not just an economic text but also one of political economy: he posits a relationship between, on the one hand, the emergence of the North East as an area economically distinct from the rest of Italy and, on the other, Italy's entrenched subcultures, in the sense that the areas of the 'Third Italy' are primarily Catholic ('white') or communist ('red') areas.

The discovery of the 'Third Italy' spawned a new research agenda (in Italy and elsewhere) on flexible specialisation in production methods, the dynamism of small firms in advanced economies, and the socio-political and cultural underpinning of these areas. Bagnasco and Carlo Triglia (the person with whom he began the research in the mid-1970s) produced, between them, a further three (more specialised) volumes which investigate further the origins, working and nature of the political and economic relationships in the Third Italy. Two of these are jointly edited case studies: *Società e politica nelle aree di piccola impresa: il caso di Bassano* (1984) [4.19] (in the Veneto, an area dominated by the Catholic sub-culture); and *Società e politica nelle aree di piccola impresa: il caso di Valdelsa* (1985) [4.20] (in Tuscany, an area dominated by the Marxist sub-culture). The third, by Carlo Triglia, is a comparative analysis of the two areas, which attempts to identify the manner in which the sub-cultures influence economic development in the respective areas: *Grandi partiti e piccole imprese. Comunisti e democristiani nelle regioni a economia diffusa* (1986) [4.56]. The collection edited by Marino Regini, *La sfida della flessibilità* (1988) [4.51] shows the general range and depth of the research produced on flexible specialisation.

There has also been some good work produced in English. Indeed, Michael J. Piore and Charles F. Sabel, *The Second Industrial Divide: Possibilities for Prosperity* (1984) [4.49] uses mainly Italian examples of flexible specialisation as a means of promoting a general European debate on state support strategies and industrial policies. Similarly, Linda Weiss, *Creating Capitalism: the State and Small Business since 1945* (1988) [4.60] focuses primarily on the flourishing of the small economy in Italy. This is a result, she argues, of a specific strategy of state support which can be contrasted with the more 'corporatist' strategies of Northern Europe. Edward Goodman and Julia Bamford, *Small Firms and Industrial Districts in Italy* (1991) [4.34] highlights the importance of small firms and their political environments in Italy, and is largely positive about the industrial district model of economic development. Frank Pyke, Giacomo Becattini and Werner Sengenberger (eds), *Industrial Districts and Inter-Firm Co-operation in Italy* (1990) [4.50] is the product of an international research project organised by the International Institute for Labour Studies in Geneva. It is rich with material and includes more skeptical and critical evaluations of the advantages of flexible specialisation in Italy. Similarly critical (although more controversial in its methodology) is Michael Blim's case study of small firms in the shoe industry in a town in the Marche, *Made in Italy: Small Scale Industrialization and its Consequences* (1990) [4.23].

Finally, Raffaella Nanetti, *Growth and Territorial Policies. The Italian Model of Social Capitalism* (1988) [4.45], combines and develops the research on the Third Italy with that which has been produced on regionalisation (see Chapter 3, section on sub-national government and centre-periphery relations) to produce a conceptually innovative model of the Italian political economy. She posits a correlation between economic diffusion and institutional decentralisation (which in Italy were occurring simultaneously in the 1970s) and argues that the relationship between the two has a distinct temporal dimension in so far as they mutually reinforce each other. She uses this correlation to explain Italy's unexpected success in responding to the economic crisis of the 1970s: a unique response characterised by differentiated policies initiated and managed by sub-national governments which she defines as a model of 'social capitalism' and which she distinguishes from the 'welfare state'.

The literature on flexible specialisation and industrial districts emphasises the importance of informal cooperation and linkages between firms as a recipe for success. Yet, it should not be overlooked that Italy has a strong tradition in some areas (e.g. Emilia Romagna) of groups of firms formally organised along cooperative lines. Broad overviews of the cooperative movement and its importance, particularly to the Italian communists, are provided by I. Bianco, *Il movimento cooperativo italiano. Storia e ruolo nell'economia nazionale* (1975) [4.22], and Guido Bonfante et al., *Il movimento cooperativo in Italia* (1981) [4.26]. In English, John Earle, *The Italian Cooperative Movement: a Portrait of the Lega delle Cooperative e Mutue* (1986) [4.32] is a good historical introduction to one of the cooperative associations in Italy, and Mark Holmstrom, *Industrial Democracy in Italy: Workers' Co-ops and the Self-Management Debate* (1989) [4.39] is a case study of workers' cooperatives in Emilia Romagna. For those conducting research in this area, the two volumes of documents and writings edited by Walter Briganti are an indispensable resource: *Il movimento cooperativo in Italia, 1926-1962. Scritti e documenti* (1978) [4.27], and *Il movimento cooperativo in italia, 1963-1980. Scritti e documenti* (1981) [4.28].

POLITICAL ECONOMY

The study of political economy has remained a relatively undeveloped field in Italy, but has nonetheless made great strides in recent years, not only through the development of sophisticated analyses of territorial development (as outlined in the section immediately above), but also through the adoption of comparative methods of political economic analysis to examine the Italian case.

A useful evaluation of the field and its application to Italy is provided in Giuliano Urbani (ed), *Politica ed economia. Fenomeni politici e analisi economiche* (1987) [4.76]. The product of a conference on the state of political science in Italy organised in 1984 by the Feltrinelli Foundation, the volume consists of seven chapters written by economists and political scientists, who investigate the methodological and theoretical problems in combining political and economic analysis and the utility of economic models in the analysis of political phenomena. The volume is not dedicated entirely to an analysis of the Italian case but several of the chapters use Italy as a case study to illuminate their arguments, and the volume therefore provides a valuable resource for political economists.

A similarly valuable comparative work is Giovanni Arrighi (ed), *Semiperipheral Development: The Politics of Southern Europe in the Twentieth Century* (1985) [4.61]. This volume explores whether the countries of Southern Europe (the 'semiperiphery') have experienced a common pattern of political-economic development which distinguishes them from the countries of Northern Europe (the 'core'). Italy emerges as an anomalous case (neither of the core or the semiperiphery), summarised in Peter Lange's notion of the country being at the 'perimeter of the core.' In similar vein, Ray Hudson and Jim Lewis (eds), *Uneven Development in Southern Europe: Studies of Accumulation, Class, Migration and the State* (1985) [4.68], conceptualise the development of the southern European countries within a common framework.

For works concentrating just on Italy, Vittorio Valli, *Politica economica: I modelli, gli strumenti, l'economia italiana* (1992) [4.77] is a basic guide and is regularly up-dated (the 1992 version is the third edition). Several works on Italian political economy, from the 1970s onwards, gained prominence through their articulation of distinctive arguments concerning the role of the 'regime party', the Christian Democrats (DC). Building on his earlier important study of industrial policy (*Il governo dell'industria* (1971) [3.80]) Giuliano Amato produced the first significant general characterisation of the relationship between the economic and political systems, *Economia, politica e istituzioni* (1976) [3.81]. Through an analysis of three key sectors (agriculture, industry and public expenditure), Amato argues that government intervention has had little to do with directing or controlling processes at work, but rather responding to a diverse range of interests and demands which have been nurtured by the long-term presence of the DC in government and by the failure of the strategies of the trade unions and opposition parties. The basis of Italian political economy is, then, a 'spoils-distributing' government (*governo spartitorio*).

Giorgio Galli and A. Nannei, *Il capitalismo assistenziale. Ascesa e declino del sistema economico italiano 1960-1975* (1976) [4.65] argues that the DC represents the 'state bourgeoisie', a sector which is the prime beneficiary of public expenditure and exercises most influence over it. In similar vein, the best historical work is Michele Salvati, *Economia e politica dal dopoguerra a oggi* (1984) [4.73], which unravels the relationship between the distortions in Italy's postwar economic development and the political role of the DC and the effects of this in terms of the crisis of the 1970s and Italy's response to it (decentralising production and expanding the 'black' economy). A more up to date account of the development and crisis of the Italian economy is Giulio Sapelli, *Sul capitalismo italiano. Trasformazione e declino* (1993) [4.74]. The best thematic work in English is undoubtedly Peter Lange and Marino Regini (eds), *State, Market, and Social Regulation. New Perspectives on Italy* (1989) [4.69], which deals with regulation of the economy, industrial relations and the welfare state. By use of an excellent theoretical-comparative framework, the book evaluates the influence of different forms of state and social regulation (the market, community and large interest groups).

There are several works which concentrate more specifically on economic policies and policy-making. Mario Monti, *Il governo dell'economia e della moneta* (1992) [4.70] provides a general overview of economic policy-making. Two good books specifically analyse monetary and tax policies: Francesco Spinelli and Giuseppe Tullio (eds), *Monetary Policy, Fiscal Policy and Economic Activity: the Italian Experience* (1983) [4.75]; and Antonio Pedone, *Evasori e tartassati: i nodi della politica tributaria italiana* (1979) [4.71], the latter being a more genuine work of political economy, emphasising, as it does, policy failures in terms of political pressures on policy-makers. An understanding of budget's structure and process is provided by Sergio Gambale, *Struttura e ruolo del bilancio dello Stato in Italia* (1980) [4.67]. Public debt has been a feature of Italian economic life since the 1970s. It is analysed in three good works: Francesco Giavazzi and Luigi Spaventa, *High Public Debt: the Italian Experience* (1988) [4.66]; Franco Bruni (ed), *Debito pubblico e politica economica in Italia* (1987) [4.62]; and F. Cavazutti, *Debito pubblico e ricchezza privata* (1986) [4.63].

The single institution which has retained a degree of autonomy from political parties and whose operations have been fundamental to the fortunes of the Italian economy is the Bank of Italy. A. Finocchiaro and A.M. Contessa (eds), *La Banca d'Italia e i problemi del governo della moneta* (1986) [4.64] and G. Puccini, *L'autonomia della Banca d'Italia* (1978) [4.72] provide good overviews of the development of the Bank of Italy, its contemporary role, and its degree of autonomy from, and (often fractious) relations with, the Italian political system.

44   Survey and Analysis

LABOUR MARKET AND INTEREST GROUPS

The structure of the labour market is analysed in several works among which Massimo Paci (ed), *Stato, mercato, e occupazione* (1985) [4.102], Corrado Barberis, *La società italiana: redditi, occupazione, imprese* (1985) [4.82], and Franco Ferrarotti (ed), *Mercato del lavoro, marginalità sociale, e struttura di classe* (1978) [4.91] are particularly noteworthy. They emphasise the fragmentation of the labour market, the persistence of small firms and the absence of government regulation of parts of it. Michele Bruni and Loretta De Luca, *Unemployment and Labour Market Flexibility* (1994) [4.84] analyses unemployment in Italy and emphasises the role played by the coexistence of inefficient and competitive sectors of the economy. This is the best book to have appeared on this subject and provides a critical understanding to the dynamics of the labour market. This last point (the development of the so-called 'black economy') is analysed in detail in Bruno Contini, *Lo sviluppo di un economia parallela: la segmentazione del mercato del lavoro in Italia e la crescita del settore irregolare* (1979) [4.88]. Mention should also be made of Charles Sabel, *Work and Politics. The division of labor in industry* (1982) [4.108]. This is a comparative work which is essential reading for those wishing to understand how militant industrial action occurs and its effects on the nature of the industrial and social system in Italy (particularly through diversification).

William Tousijn (ed), *Le libere professioni in Italia* (1987) [4.109] is one of the few books which provides an overview of the professions in Italy. It contains two general chapters followed by seven informative chapters on specific Italian professional groupings: lawyers, notaries, journalists, medics, agronomists, veterinarians, biologists, chemists, geologists and so on. Many of the chapters provide good historical analyses of the origins of professionalisation of the occupations and the nature and impact of this trend.

The study of interest groups in Italy has been hampered by the failure of industrial relations to develop fully as an object of historical enquiry and the dominance of legal scholars in the field. This has meant that some of the best work in this small field has been carried out by foreign scholars. The classic treatment of interest groups in Italy remains Joseph LaPalombara, *Interest Groups in Italian Politics* (1964) [4.98]. Its thesis of two modes of interest group mediation with the state -- *clientela* and *parentela* -- influenced a whole generation of research. Its 1980s equivalent (in terms of required reading) is Peter Lange and Marino Regini, *State, Market and Social Regulation: New Perspectives on Italy* [4.69]. Leonardo Morlino (ed), *Costruire la democrazia: Gruppi e partiti in Italia* (1991) [4.101] is a good collection of articles on the relationship between interest groups and the political parties. Piero Trupia, *La democrazia degli interessi: lobby e decisione collettiva* (1989) [4.110] is a useful analysis of the organisational capacity of Italian interest groups and their influence in the political system. The best overall perspective on the industrial relations system is provided by Gian Primo Cella and Tiziano Treu (eds), *Le relazioni industriali* (1982) [4.86]. The best work in English is provided by A. Ferner and R. Hyman in a substantial 76 page chapter on Italy in their edited work, *Industrial Relations in the New Europe* (1992) [4.90].

The key interest groups representing business and labour have received mixed treatment. There is no book length study in English of Confindustria and Italian business associations, and a limited amount of good literature in Italian. The two most recent accounts are Luca Lanzalaco, *Lo sviluppo organizzativo delle associazioni imprenditoriali. Il caso della Confindustria* (1992) [4.97], and Liborio Mattina, *Gli industriali e la democrazia: la Confindustria nella formazione dell'Italia repubblicana* (1992) [4.100] (the latter of which explores particularly well the relationship with the DC). Also of note are Gloria Pirzio Ammassari, *La politica della Confindustria: strategia economica e prassi contrattuale del padronato italiano* (1976) [4.103], and AA.VV, *La politica del padronato italiano* (1972) [4.78]. Useful material can also be found in Fondazione Giovanni Agnelli, *Il sistema imprenditoriale italiano* (1974) [4.93] and in the archival work put together under the auspices of *Confindustria* and edited by Oreste Bazziche and Riccardo Vommaro, *Guida all'archivio storico confindustria: 1910-1990* (1990) [4.87].

Studies on the Italian labour movement are more numerous than those on business. Research has generally been influenced by Italy's characteristic of 'labour exclusion', where the major component of the union movement has been excluded from effective political participation in the state because of its communism and the movement has consequently been divided. Joanne Barkan, *Visions of Emancipation: the Italian Workers' Movement Since 1945* (1984) [4.83], is a good introduction to the subject. Several books provide analyses of the development of trade union strategies in the postwar period. Aris Accornero, *La parabola del sindacato. Ascesa e declino di una cultura* (1992) [4.79] examines the distinctive characteristics of the Italian trade union experience and explains its rise and decline in the context of its strategy of pursuing wage egalitarianism from the late 1960s onwards. It is arguably the best account available of the development of the trade union movement.

Peter Lange, George Ross and Maurizio Vannicelli (eds), *Unions, Change and Crisis: French and Italian Union Strategy and the Political Economy, 1945-1980* (1984) [4.96] is the product of a research project of the Center for European Studies at Harvard University on postwar trade union strategies of the Italian and French labour movements. Umberto Romagnolo and Tiziano Treu, *I sindacati in Italia: storia di una strategia (1945-1976)* (1977) [4.107] provides a good overview of trade union strategy until the mid-1970s. Miriam Golden, *Labor Divided: Austerity and Working-Class Politics in Contemporary Italy* (1988) [4.95] is an analysis (based on a wealth of data and personal interviews) of the trade unions during the period of austerity (the mid-1970s), and seeks to explain why some unions operated a moderate policy while others took a more militant line. C. Baglioni, *Il sindacato dell'autonomia: l'evoluzione della CGIL nella pratica e nella cultura* (1977) [4.80] is a study of the development of the most significant of the trade unions, the socialist-communist dominated General Confederation of Labour (*Confederazione generale italiano del lavoro*).

Worker militancy until the 1970s is analysed by Vittorio Foa (ed), *Sindacati e lotte operaie (1943-1973)* [4.92]. The militancy of the late 1960s constituted an important watershed in the industrial relations system and prompted considerable research. The four volumes produced by Alessandro Pizzorno et al., *Lotte operaie e sindacato in Italia (1968-1972)* (1974) [4.104] provides the most extensive coverage. The response of industry is documented in a comparative assessment with the French experience in A. Gigliobianco and M. Salvati, *Il maggio francese e l'autunno caldo italiano: la risposta di due borghesie* (1980) [4.94]. Gian Primo Cella and Marino Regini (eds), *Il conflitto industriale in Italia. Stato della ricerca e ipotesi sulle tendenze* (1985) [4.85] and Marino Regini, *I dilemmi del sindacato. Conflitto e partecipazione negli anni settanta e ottanta* (1981) [4.105] both provide good material and articles on industrial conflict in Italy in the 1970s and 1980s.

The defeat of the trade unions in the Fiat strike of 1980s is viewed as a further watershed in Italian industrial relations and is the subject of Marco Revelli, *Lavorare in Fiat da Valetta ad Agnelli a Romiti: operai, sindacati, robot* (1989) [4.106]. Revelli places the strike and its defeat in the context of the development of the Mirafiori works in the 1950s and 1960s and its restructuring in the 1970s (and, after the strike, in the 1980s). A. Baldissera, *La rivolta dei quarantamila: dai quadri FIAT ai COBAS* (1988) [4.81] analyses the strike and the decline in control exercised by trade union leaders over militants, evidenced in the growth of the so-called COBAS (*comitati di base*, grassroots committees). The clash over the wage-indexation system (*scala mobile*) in 1984 was another milestone in worker militancy which divided the trade union movement down the middle. Raffaella Lungarella, *La scala mobile 1945-1981: caratteristiche, storia, problemi* (1981) [4.99] gives a good history of the wage indexation system until the end of the 1970s, including the extension of the scope of indexation to one hundred per cent in 1975 which became the source of conflict in the 1980s. A. di Gioia, *La scala mobile* (1984) [4.89], outlines the background to the 1984 conflict and the referendum which eventually determined the cut in wage indexation which occurred.

ENTREPRENEURS

It is apparent from this chapter that Italy's business culture varies considerably depending on the size of the firms and their territorial location, but mention should be made of a more general debate concerning this issue: the difference between the public and private sectors. In 1974 two leading journalists, Eugenio Scalfari and Giuseppe Turani, produced what was to become a best-selling book in Italy, *Razza padrona. Storia della borghesia di stato* (1974) [4.116], whose essential thesis was the contrast, if not contradiction, between the dynamic forces of Italy's private enterprise, led by a number of key individuals, and the sluggishness and loss-making economic activities of the public sector.

This thesis has not gone uncontested, but it points to an important Italian phenomenon: the significance of, and power wielded by, a number of top Italian entrepreneurs in both the private and the public, or semi-public, sectors who will often use unorthodox practices to achieve success and influence the top echelons of government. Indeed, no knowledge of the distribution of political and economic power in Italy would be complete without a knowledge of the ways and means of these key individuals. Fortunately, there are some good case studies in Italian and English on these people. Giuseppe Berta, *Le idee al potere: Adriano Olivetti tra la fabbrica e la Comunità* (1980) [4.111], and D. Ronci, *Olivetti, anni 50* (1980) [4.115], provide accounts of Adriano Olivetti and his typewriter factory at Ivrea, one of the great success stories of the 1950s. P. Frankel, *Mattei: Oil and Power Politics* (1966) [4.113] and Dow Votaw, *The Six-Legged Dog: Mattei and ENI -- A Study in Power* (1964) [4.118] show how Enrico Mattei built up an industrial empire within the state sector through his control of the state petrol company, AGIP, and later the holding company, ENI (which diversified into a myriad of industrial activities), and how he used this base to build up a political network inside the DC. Alan Friedman, *Agnelli and the Network of Italian Power* (1988) [4.114] is a controversial account of Italy's wealthiest man and the nation's largest employer, the Fiat magnate, Gianni Agnelli. The author paints Fiat as a network of power which is not so different in structure to the Mafia but which uses different methods to violence to crush any opposition to it. The change in Fiat's strategy under Agnelli away from the cosy relationship it enjoyed (under Valletta) with the DC is analysed in V. Comito, *La FIAT tra crisi e ristrutturazione* (1982) [4.112]. Lastly, G. Turani, *L'Ingegnere* (1988) [4.117] is an account of De Benedetti, the industrialist who worked briefly for Fiat and then became head of Olivetti and the first Italian businessman to stand up to the Agnelli regime.

5

Society

GENERAL WORKS

For those beginning their studies on Italy and for the educated general reader there are several basic introductions to Italian society and the Italian people. Russell King, *Italy* (1987) [5.15] is a useful socio-geographic analysis of the country (which also includes political and economic aspects). Entertaining introductory reading is provided in: John Haycraft, *Italian Labyrinth. Italy in the 1980s* (1987) [5.16]; Michael Caesar and Peter R. Hainsworth, *Writers and Society in Contemporary Italy* (1984) [5.8]; Luigi Barzini, *The Italians* (1991) [5.6]; Charles Richards, *The New Italians* (1995) [5.24]. William Ward, *Getting it Right in Italy. A Manual for the 1990s* (1990) [5.26] is an ideal guide and introduction to those working or living in the country.

The most complete analyses of Italy's social structure are provided by Sabino S. Acquaviva and M. Santuccio, *Social Structure in Italy: Crisis of a System* (1976) [5.2]; Massimo Paci, *La struttura sociale italiano: costanti storiche e trasformazioni recenti* (1982) [5.19]; and Paci's more recent *Il mutamento della struttura sociale in Italia* (1992) [5.20]. Many will find Acquaviva and Santuccio's book hard going because of its (at times) abstract language and its thesis of a structural crisis in the social system, but some of the features the work identifies are useful to understanding contemporary Italian society. The book also has a good bibliography. Paci's work analyses Italian social structures in terms of the effects upon them of the small-business sector, economic factors common to advanced capitalist democracies and the political system. Part Two of Donald Sassoon, *Contemporary Italy* [2.21] provides the best introduction to the pervading themes of Italian society and the essential debates in the literature, although Paul Ginsborg, *A History of Contemporary Italy* [1.7] provides the best analysis in historical context.

Luisa Quartermaine and John Pollard (eds), *Italy Today: Patterns of Life and Politics* (1985) [5.23] is an interesting, if disparate, collection of writings on aspects of Italian society. More rewarding is the collection edited by Ugo Ascoli and Raimondo Catanzaro, *La società italiana degli anni Ottantà* (1987) [5.1] and Corrado Barberis, *La società italiana. Esperienze di un secolo* (1992) [5.4]. The most comprehensive statistical surveys of Italian society are provided in regular reports by ISTAT [5.17] and CENSIS [5.9] (condensed versions of which are also available in English) and in a comprehensive annual report by Eurispes (the *Istituto di Studi Politici, Economici e Sociali*), *Rapporto Italia* [5.10]. For a flavour of the work of Italian sociologists, Diana Pinto (ed), *Contemporary Italian Sociology* (1981) [5.22] is to be recommended, although it is hard going at times for those unversed in sociological analysis. It represents the best work of the radical school of Italian sociologists who refute the idea of the 'specificity' of the Italian crisis of the 1970s.

The considerable literature on popular culture in countries such as Britain, America and Australia is hardly equalled in work on Italy. The study of Italian mass and popular culture has suffered both from the preoccupation (particularly marked amongst foreigners), with Italian literary and architectural 'high' or elite culture, and from the narrowness of the history and political science disciplines which have tended to overlook the analysis of popular culture (apart from the analysis of political and cultural production in the Fascist period). Guido Barlozzini and Marcello Beltramme (eds), *1945-1970. Società, politica, cultura in Italia* (1976) [5.5] is a rare example of good early work.

Recent research goes some way towards filling this gap. The most impressive book is Giovanni Bechelloni (ed), *Il mutamento culturale in Italia (1945-1985)* (1989) [5.7] which brings together 35 specialists of cultural processes (many of them sociologists) who analyse virtually every aspect of Italian culture. The best history of mass cultural changes since Unification is provided by Silvio Lanaro, *L'Italia Nuova: Identità e Sviluppo, 1861-1988* (1988) [5.18], which is impressive in its charting of the modernisation process in Italy. Another historical work, David Forgacs, *Italian Culture in the Industrial Era 1880-1980: Cultural Industries, Politics and the Public* (1990) [5.11], specifically takes issue with the traditional focus on high culture (and particularly the role of intellectuals) by arguing that the process of industrialisation (and thus the changing social structure and markets) is central to understanding cultural production in Italy. The author focuses on cinema, radio and television to unravel the process of cultural modernisation and its links with high culture, politics and the demands of industrialisation (and particularly profitability and expanding markets). Its broad sweep makes it a good introduction for English readers to the history of Italian popular culture. Robert Putnam's analysis of the historical development of different cultural patterns in *Making Democracy Work* [2.20] is also of importance here.

A more general introduction to this subject area is provided by David Forgacs and Robert Lumley (eds), *Introduction to Italian Cultural Studies* (1995) [5.12]. Zygmunt G. Baranski and Robert Lumley (eds), *Culture and Conflict in Postwar Italy. Essays on Mass and Popular Culture* (1990) [5.3] adopts a broadly based pragmatic approach to the meaning of 'popular and mass culture'. The book brings together recent research to provide an introduction to some of the cultural changes (in cinema, design, television, intellectual life and the sub-cultures) which Italy has undergone in the postwar period. Saverio Vertone (ed), *La cultura degli italiani* (1994) [5.25] is an impressive collection whose broad objective is to explore and define an Italian 'identity'. Stephen Gundle, *Italy Transformed: The Communist Party, Cultural Change and Modernization 1943-91* (1994) [5.14] explores the communist culture and the role of the party in shaping cultural change in Italy in the postwar period. Aldo Grasso, *Storia della televisione italiana* (1992) [5.13] is the first general history of Italian television from a sociological perspective. It is an important milestone in Italian media studies. Finally, Gianfranco Pasquino (ed), *Mass media e sistema politico* (1984) [5.21] provides a useful analysis of the influence of Italian politics on the nature of the mass media in Italy. Amongst other things, it shows why American models of political communication have not been useful in explaining the Italian case because of the dominance of Italian politics by parties and not personalities who are susceptible to television.

SOCIAL CLASSES AND MOVEMENTS

The literature on social classes has been dominated by the debate generated by important contributions from two authors: the sociologist, Alessandro Pizzorno, in his seminal article 'I ceti medi nel meccanismo del consenso' (1971), now contained in the excellent collection of Pizzorno's most important articles, *I soggetti del pluralismo. Classi, partiti, sindacati* (1982) [5.36]; and the economist Paolo Sylos Labini in his well-known *Saggio sulle classi sociale italiana* (1982) [5.39], originally published in 1974. Pizzorno identified the consolidation of power by the Italian ruling classes as having been based on attracting the support of the middle classes by offering them the possibility of individualistic success. Sylos Labini analysed Italy's changing social structure and concluded that, contrary to the political left's assumptions, the 'productive' middle classes in Italy were not being pauperised by the development of capitalism. They were occupying an increasingly strong position in Italian society and their interests were not compatible with those of the working class.

The debate (conducted primarily through academic journals) focused on the sources and accuracy of Sylos Labini's statistics, the respective weights of the working and middle classes and the complexity of their economic and political roles. Livio Maitan, *Dinamica delle classi sociali in Italia* (1975) [5.34], Paolo Ammassari, *Classi e ceti nella società italiana* (1977) [5.27] and Carlo Carboni, *Classe e movimento in Italia 1970-1985* (1986) [5.30] are important contributions to the debate, and mention should also be made of Corrado Barberis, *La società italiana: classi e caste nello sviluppo economico* (1976) [5.28]. Sylos Labini's later book, *Le classi sociali negli anni '80* (1986) [5.40], provides a useful overview of the debate and the modifications in the authors' own arguments. While accepting the necessity of some adjustments to his statistical analysis, the author holds to his essential thesis of the growth of the *ceti medi* as a percentage of the active population.

Academic interest in social movements was stimulated primarily by the social protest and spontaneous collective action of the late 1960s, which developed in the context of militant industrial action (see Chapter 4, section on labour market and interest groups) and which had a lasting impact on Italian politics and society. The period generated a large amount of literature, much of it too immediate and sympathetic to the militants' cause to gain any real perspective. Some of these accounts are nevertheless worth reading, and a notable example is Eugenio Scalfari, *L'autunno della Repubblica. La mappa del potere in Italia* (1969) [5.38]. Two mainstream academic studies produced in the late 1980s place the social movements of the late 1960s in a much broader perspective. Sidney Tarrow, *Democracy and Disorder: Protest and Politics in Italy, 1965-1975* (1989) [5.41], uses the concept of a protest cycle in order to analyse the origins of the social movements, their strategies and competitive nature and their outcome (whether in terms of terrorism or the return to institutional struggle). The book also makes an important contribution to the debate on the 'maturing' of Italian democracy. Robert Lumley, *States of Emergency: Cultures of Revolt in Italy from 1968 to 1978* (1989) [5.33], is more concerned with the cultural continuities between the movements of the late 1960s (primarily workers and students) and those of the late 1970s (terrorism, youth, feminism).

Arguably, the best collection of articles on the militancy of 1968 is contained in the *Annali delle Fondazione Luigi Micheletti 1968* (1969) [5.32]. A useful collection of documents on the various revolutionary groups is contained in Davide Degli Incerti (ed), *La sinistra rivoluzionaria in Italia* (1976) [5.31], but there have been very few specific studies of these groups. Exceptions are the excellent analysis of an extra-parliamentary group by Luigi Bobbio, *Lotta Continua: Storia di un organizzazione rivoluzionaria* (1988)

[2.86], Luisa Passerini's personal account, *Autoritratto di gruppo* (1988) [5.35], and Aldo Garzia's study of the Manifesto group, *Da Natta a Natta. Storia del Manifesto e del PDUP* [2.48]. Also useful is Rossana Rossanda, *L'anno degli studenti* (1968) [5.37], an informative account of the student movement, and Giuseppe Bianchi et al., *I CUB: comitati unitari di base* (1971) [5.29], an analysis of the joint committees of factory workers and revolutionary groups which were meant to develop into genuine Leninist (or Gramscian) revolutionary factory councils.

TERRORISM

The nature of the exact link between the social movements of the 1960s and the terrorist movements of the 1970s is controversial, particularly since the publication of Tarrow's work, noted above [5.41] which questions the conventional wisdom. There is little disagreement, however, that a link existed. There is also little disagreement on the significance of Italy's terrorist experience, and that it left indelible marks on politics and society. The subject has consequently attracted much attention but less rigorous academic research. Much of the literature is of a general, impressionistic and speculative nature. Three volumes by Raimondo Catanzaro and Donatella Della Porta are significant exceptions. The first two are by both edited by Catanzaro: *Ideologie, movimenti, terrorismi* (1990) [5.42], and *La politica della violenza* (1990) [5.43]; the third is written by Della Porta, *Il terrorismo di sinistra* (1990) [5.46]. They are the fruits of a research project on left and right wing terrorism begun in 1982. They examine comprehensively the sociological, political and even psychological foundations and development of terrorism in Italy. A collection of the chapters from the first two volumes has been produced in English in Raimondo Catanzaro (ed), *The Red Brigades and Left-Wing Terrorism in Italy* (1991) [5.44] and is essential reading for specialists seeking to understand the complexities of Italian terrorism.

More suitable as introductory books are: Leonard Weinberg and William Lee Eubank, *The Rise and Fall of Italian Terrorism* (1987) [5.50]; Giorgio Galli, *Storia del partito armato* (1986) [5.47]; R. C. Meade, *Red Brigades and the Story of Italian Terrorism* (1990) [5.48] (the Red Brigades were the most significant of the left wing terrorist groups); and Donatella Della Porta (ed), *Terrorismi in Italia* (1984) [5.45], the last of which is the best empirical study of Italian left-wing terrorism available. For an innovative approach to the terrorist question (based on a dramaturgic method and analysis), Robin Erica Wagner-Pacifici, *The Moro Morality Play. Terrorism as Social Drama* (1986) [1.81] is to be recommended. Philip Willan, *Puppet Masters. The Political Use of Terrorism in Italy* [5.147] is an investigation of the possibility of the involvement of the state in terrorist activities and of political manipulation of terrorism. Finally, mention should be made of Antonio Negri, a professor of philosophy at the University of Padua whose works, most particularly *Proletari e stato* (1976) [5.49], theorised and partly inspired the objectives and strategies of the *Autonomia* revolutionary youth movement of the late 1970s, and eventually led to Negri's arrest.

WOMEN AND FEMINISM

Michela De Giorgio, *Le italiane dall'Unità a oggi. Modelli culturali e comportamenti sociali* (1992) [5.58] is the first attempt at a comprehensive general history of women over the last hundred years. It focuses on the social, cultural, symbolic public and private roles and development of Italian women, but is limited by the dearth of analysis of the postwar period (contrary to the title of the book). Other useful histories include G. Ascoli et al., *La questione femminile in Italia dal '900 ad oggi* (1977) [5.51], and Gloria Chianese, *Storia sociale della donna in Italia (1800-1980)* (1980) [5.57] which concentrates on the social aspects of women's history over a 180 year period.

Zygmunt Baranski and Shirley Vinall (eds), *Women and Italy: Essays on Gender, Culture and History* (1991) [5.52] is an interesting interdisciplinary collection of essays on women's roles in work, the arts and literature, which point the way for further research. Francesca Bettio, *The Sexual Division of Labour. The Italian Case* (1988) [5.53] is one of the few works to examine in detail the characteristics of women's and men's work in Italy, emphasising the former's historically subordinate position in society and the existence of particular patterns of occupational 'sex-typing'. Lesley Caldwell, *Italian Family Matters: Women, Politics and Legal Reform* (1991) [5.56] documents the legislation passed on women and the family. M. Weber, *Il voto delle donne* (1977) [5.62] analyses the nature, patterns and significance of women's voting.

More specifically on feminism, Lucia Chiavola Birnbaum, *Liberazione della donna: Feminism in Italy* (1986) [5.54] provides an historical overview of the last thirty years, although it will be laborious and too detailed for many readers. Judith Hellman, *Journeys Among Women* (1987) [5.59] is an exceptionally good study of the feminist movement in different cities and regions. The diversity she discovers between cities and regions demonstrates the value of a comparative analysis of a social movement (most tend to be focused on either one region or city). Rosa Rossi, *Le parole delle donne* (1978) [5.61] is an interesting analysis of feminist speech and campaign slogans. Paola Bono and Sandra Kemp (eds), *Italian Feminist Thought: A Reader* (1991) [5.55] provides key translated writings of Italian feminist thinkers, and includes a useful bibliography and list of women's centres. Finally, Maria Cristina Marcuzzo and Anna Rossi-Doria (eds), *La ricerca delle donne: studi femministi in Italia* (1987) [5.60] provides a useful overview of feminist studies in Italy for those beginning their research.

FAMILY AND YOUTH

The Italian family and working class life have provided important areas of research and debate, particularly because of the continued importance of the family in Italy and the fact that it resists easy characterisation (a product of the differences between family life in the North and South). Much of the early work - largely by anthropologists - was focused on the South and the peasantry, a consequence of Edward Banfield's book, *The Moral Basis of a Backward Society* (1958) [5.67] in which he forwarded his controversial - and hotly disputed - thesis of 'amoral familism'. Indeed, North American anthropology of Italy became almost obsessive in its focus on this debate in the period until the 1970s, to the neglect of researching other important areas. The best summary of the literature generated by this thesis is the Italian edition of Banfield's book (edited by Domenico De Masi), *Le basi morali di una società arretrata* (1976) [5.68] which contains a selection of the key contributions in the debate. An important book-length contribution on this subject is Pierpaolo Donati, *Pubblico e privato, fine di un alternativa?* (1978) [5.77] which argues that familism has not dominated Italian life; rather, there have been times when family interests and collective interests have been closely integrated.

More recent accounts of rural family life have been less contentious than Banfield's. Donald S. Pitkin, *The House that Giacomo Built* (1985) [5.80] successfully links the history of three generations of a family and its values to more general political, social and economic changes, thus showing the effects of economic development on rural family life. Roland Sarti, *Long Live the Strong: A History of Rural Society in the Apennine*

Mountains (1985) [5.81] is one of the few general surveys of rural life in the Apennines over the last hundred years. Bianca Barbero Avanzini and Clemente Lanzetti, *Problemi e modelli di vita familiare. Una ricerca in ambito urbano* (1980) [5.69] is a study of urban family life. Based on interviews with married couples living in Milan in 1976, it reveals, echoing Banfield on rural life in the South, the low levels of interest in issues beyond the family even in urban areas in the mid-1970s.

The best overviews of the Italian family are provided by Piero Melograni (ed), *La famiglia italiana dall'Ottocento a oggi* (1988) [5.79], and Laura Balbo, *Stato di Famiglia* (1976) [5.66]. Mention should also be made of David I. Kertzer and Richard P. Saller (eds), *The Family in Italy. From Antiquity to the Present* (1991) [5.78] which brings together several distinguished writers on the family. However, despite the sub-title's reference to 'the present', there is little analysis beyond the nineteenth century. AA.VV, *Ritratto di famiglia degli anni '80* (1981) [5.63] assesses the impact of the 1970s on the family. Marzio Barbagli, *Sotto lo stesso tetto: mutamenti della famiglia in Italia dal XV al XX secolo* (1984) [5.70] is an impressive analysis of the changes in family structure in the North and Centre; and his *Provando e riprovando: matrimonio, famiglia e divorzio in Italia e in altri paesi occidentali* (1990) [5.71] is the only text to deal comprehensively with the impact of legal divorce on the Italian family. A. Coletti, *Il divorzio in Italia. Storia di una battaglia civile e democratica* (1974) [5.76] is also a useful account of the divorce issue, although now rather dated. Lesley Caldwell, *Italian Family Matters: Women, Politics and Legal Reform* [5.56] documents the legislation which has had an impact on the family.

Youth became a significant phenomenon in the late 1960s and 1970s, when societal changes had a significant impact on young people and sociologists began to study them as an independent 'class' of people with their own life-style and demands. Two books examine the impact of this critical period: Francesco Alberoni, *Classi e generazioni* (1970) [5.64], and P. Bassi and A. Pilati, *I giovani e la crisi degli anni settanta* (1978) [5.72]. This change in the status of youth as a field of study was reflected in the commencement, in 1980, of a project which has continued since and has resulted in three significant publications, known as the Iard reports: Alessandro Cavalli, V. Cesarea, Antonio de Lillo, L. Ricolfi, G. Romagnoli, *Giovanni oggi. Indagine Iard sulla condizione giovanile in Italia* (1984) [5.73]; Alessandro Cavalli and Antonio de Lillo, *Giovanni anni '80* (1988) [5.74]; and Alessandro Cavalli and Antonio de Lillo (eds), *Giovanni anni '90. Terzo rapport Iard sulla condizione giovanile in Italia* (1995) [5.75]. The project examines the condition of Italian youth and is based on wide-ranging interviews for each volume in all regions of the country. The three volumes together provide a broad panorama of change over a fifteen year period. Finally, mention should be made of a similar study but one with a longer time span. Using a 1954 survey of youth carried out by the Christian Association of Italian Workers (ACLI), Percy Allum and Ilvo Diamanti adopted a similar methodology to analyse young people in the 1980s, and then compared the results of each. Their findings are produced in *'50/'80, vent'anni. Due generazioni di giovanni a confronto* (1986) [5.65], a comparison of two generations which broadens into providing a revealing picture of socio-cultural change over a twenty-five year period.

CHURCH AND RELIGION

In view of its considerable (but declining) influence on the development of postwar Italian society and politics, research on the church has not been bountiful. There have been few in depth studies of the political role of the Vatican and church-state relations in general since the publication of A. C. Jemolo, *Church and State in Italy 1850-1950* (1960) [5.90] and Vincent P. Bucci, *Chiesa e stato: Church-State Relations in Italy within the Contemporary Constitutional Framework* (1969) [5.82]. Alfonso Prandi's analysis of the political influence of the church, *Chiesa e politica* (1968) [5.97], was published in the same period. Of recent research, Andrea Riccardi's historical analysis of the Pope's power and influence is to be recommended: *Il potere del papa. Da Pio XII a Giovanni Paolo II* (1993) [5.101]. A good collection of historical analyses of the church's influence is contained in G. Chittolini and Giovanni Miccoli (eds), *Storia d'Italia, Annali IX: la Chiesa e il potere dal Medioevo all'età contemporanea* (1986) [5.85]. A general overview of the church's role in the first thirty years of the Republic is provided by Giacomo Martina, *La chiesa in Italia negli ultimi trent'anni* (1979) [5.93].

The role played by the Vatican in the 1940s and 1950s was critical to the future of organised Catholicism in the new Republic and is examined by Andrea Riccardi, *Il 'partito romano' nel secondo dopoguerra (1945-1954)* (1983) [5.99]. Also useful is Riccardi's edited collection on Pius XII (Eugenio Pacelli, Pope from 1939-1958): *Pio XII* (1984) [5.100]. The Vatican's policy in the postwar period of promoting the growth of Catholic organisations in society is examined by C. Falconi, *La chiesa e le organizzazioni cattoliche in Italia (1945-1955)* (1956) [5.88]. The role of the largest of these, Catholic Action, is analysed by Gianfranco Poggi, *Catholic Action in Italy* (1967) [5.95]. A more general account of organised catholicism is provided by Giorgio Candeloro, *Il movimento cattolico in Italia* (1982) [5.84]. Mention should also be made of the *Dizionario storico del movimento cattolico in Italia 1860-1980* (1981-1984) [5.86] which, in three volumes, covers ideas, facts, protagonists and other key personalities in the Catholic movement.

On the role of the Church up to the 1960s the best account is provided by D. Settembrini, *La chiesa nella politica italiana (1944-1963)* (1977) [5.102]. The best treatment of Vatican policies and the changes which these underwent under John XXIII and Paul VI is S. Magister, *La politica vaticana e l'Italia, 1943-78* (1979) [5.92]. John XXIII's papacy was probably the most significant in the postwar era in beginning the process of *aggiornamento* ('modernisation') of the Catholic church. Peter Hebblethwaite, *Pope John XXIII: Shepherd of the Modern World* (1986) [5.89] is a good biography. David Yallop, *In God's Name. An Investigation into the Murder of Pope John Paul I* (1985) [5.103] was not, as the front cover has it, 'The book which shook the world' but is nevertheless worthwhile reading for some of its insights into Vatican politics. The views of Pope John Paul II on, amongst other things, the Papacy, the current state of the Catholic religion and the world are found in Pope John Paul II, *Crossing the Threshold of Hope* (1994) [5.96], a book which is presented in the form of an interview by Vittorio Messori.

There are few works which attempt to analyse Italian religious attitudes and behaviour at a national level. Silvano Burgalassi, *Il comportamento religioso degli italiani* (1967) [5.83] is an exception, as is C. Prandi, *La religione popolare fra potere e tradizione* (1983) [5.98]. This book also attempts to get to the heart of what exactly constitutes 'popular religion' in Italy. Beyond these books, one is dependent on local studies such as Caroline White, *Patrons and Partisans: A Study of Politics in Two Southern Italian Communities* (1980) [2.159], R. H. Evans, *Life and Politics in a Venetian Community* (1976) [5.87], and David Kertzer, *Comrades and Christians. Religion and Political Struggle in Italy* (1980) [5.91]. This last book is a good portrayal of Italian working class city life, showing how communist structures, institutions and rituals outplay their religious equivalents. It can be usefully read alongside a longer (and methodologically less refined) book by Belden Paulson (with Athos Ricci), *The Searchers. Conflict and Communism in an Italian Town* (1966) [5.94]. It need hardly be stressed that several works on Christian Democracy (cited in Chapter 2, section on political parties: individual studies) are also relevant here.

EMIGRATION AND DEMOGRAPHIC CHANGES

A complete knowledge of the development of postwar Italy is not possible without an understanding of the significant demographic changes which have occurred through emigration, internal migration and return migration. There is now a vast literature on this subject, but an absence of a comprehensive study in English. The first part of Russell King, *Il Ritorno in Patria: Return Migration to Italy in Historical Perspective* (1988) [5.113] provides an overall synthesis in English of the different historical phases of immigration.[1] In Italian, the best overviews are provided by: Vittorio Briani, *Il lavoro italiano all'estero negli ultimi cento anni* (1970) [5.105]; Gianfausto Rosoli (ed), *Un secolo di emigrazione italiana 1876-1976* (1978) [5.116]; and Ugo Ascoli, *Movimenti migratori in Italia* (1979) [5.104].

Some of the best work in this field are case studies of individual towns, localities and districts or regions. There are many of these studies, the bulk of them concentrated on the South of Italy, from where most of the emigration occurred. Of note are: Emilio Reyneri, *La catena migratoria* (1979) [5.115]; William A. Douglass, *Emigration in a South Italian Town* (1984) [5.109]; Dino Cinel, *From Italy to San Francisco: The Immigrant Experience* (1982) [5.106]; Anna Cornelisen, *Flight From Torregreca: Strangers and Pilgrims* (1980) [5.108]; and, on a Northern region, Elena Saraceno, *Emigrazione e rientri: il Friuli-Venezia Giulia nel secondo dopoguerra* (1981) [5.117]. With regard to destinations, the vast majority of studies focus on Italian migration to the United States, of which Cinel's work cited above [5.106] is only one example. The life of postwar Italian immigrants in other countries has received much less attention. Regarding internal migratory destinations, Goffredo Fofi, *L'immigrazione meridionale a Torino* (1964) [5.110] is a good case study of the effects of the migration of southerners to the northern industrial city of Turin.

Italian return migration has been the subject of extensive research. Russell King's work has already been cited above [5.113], the second part of which provides a major review of the literature on Italian return migration. Mention should also be made of his edited comparative volume, *Return Migration and Regional Economic Problems* (1986) [5.112] which has three good chapters on Italy. Joseph Lopreato, *Peasants No More* (1967) [5.114] was one of the first works in this field, examining the impact of return migration to the Italian south. Other works of note include: Maria Luisa Gentileschi and Ricciarda Simoncelli (eds), *Rientro degli emigrati e territorio* (1983) [5.111]; Amalia Signorelli, Maria-Clara Tirritico and Sara Rossi, *Scelte senza potere: il ritorno degli emigrati nelle zone di esodo* (1977) [5.119]; and Stephanie Lindsay Thompson, *Australia Through Italian Eyes: A Study of Settlers Returning from Australia to Italy* (1980) [5.120].

By the early 1980s Italy was no longer a net exporter of labour and was experiencing, in the major cities, the problems of accommodating immigrant labour, most of it from the Third World. The last ten years has consequently witnessed a new focus in much of the writing on immigration, although there has been little sustained research produced in book form. Two books which deal reasonably well with this phenomenon are N. Sergi and F. Carchedi (eds), *L'immigrazione straniera in Italia* (1992) [5.118] and G. Cocchi (ed), *Stranieri in Italia* (1990) [5.107].

MAFIA AND THE UNDERWORLD

The Mafia has always been an interesting, if difficult, field of research for sociologists, anthropologists, historians and others. The late 1980s made the area even more fertile with the amount of material made available from parliamentary commissions, the so-called maxi-trial of hundreds of suspected *mafiosi*, the revelations of *pentiti* (those who 'grassed' in return for reduced sentences) and the exposure by the judiciary of the links between the Mafia and politicians at both the local and national levels. There is now a considerable amount of literature on this subject in English as well as Italian.

Three outstanding historical works on the Mafia by North American anthropologists in the 1970s are still essential texts: Henner Hess, *Mafia* (1973) [5.136], which is probably the classic history of the Mafia up to the 1960s; Peter and Jane Schneider, *Culture and Political Economy in Western Sicily* (1976) [5.142]; and Anton Blok, *The Mafia of a Sicilian Village 1860-1960. A Study of Violent Peasant Entrepreneurs* (1988) [5.124]. The most complete history of the Mafia from its origins until the contemporary period is Salvatore Lupo, *Storia della Mafia dalle origini ai giorni nostri* (1993) [5.137].

On the Mafia in the postwar period, and particularly its transformation into a system of capitalistic enterprises, the best analyses are: Pino Arlacchi, *Mafia Business: The Mafia Ethic and the Spirit of Capitalism* (1987) [5.122], which is a synthesis of the work carried out by the author in the late 1970s and shows the changes the Mafia underwent in that decade; Raimondo Catanzaro, *Crime as an Enterprise: A Social History of the Sicilian Mafia* (1992) [5.125]; and Diego Gambetta, *The Sicilian Mafia: The Business of Private Protection* (1994) [5.134]. All three works present the Mafia as entrepreneurial and functioning in the market in the same way as other industries, the difference being that the Mafia is a set of enterprises specialising in the supply of protection. Gambetta takes this thesis to its extreme in structuring his book clearly around the study of an industry, and showing how it has penetrated different markets such as construction, fish, fruit and vegetables.

An excellent collection which brings together nearly all of the contemporary Mafia specialists is G. Findaca and S. Costantino (eds), *La Mafia. Le Mafie* (1994) [5.132], which analyses the phenomenon from all angles and can be regarded as indispensable to researchers. Filippo Sabetti, *Political Authority in a Sicilian Village* (1984) [5.141] is a good case study which shows exactly how the Mafia establishes and exercises its control over towns and villages. James Walston, *The Mafia and Clientelism. Roads to Rome in Post War Calabria* (1988) [5.146], examines the role of the Mafia in local administration in two cities of Calabria and its impact on the distribution of public resources.

The role of the state and politicians in the development of the Mafia is best analysed in an anthology of documents brought together by Nicola Tranfaglia, *Mafia, Politica e Affari, 1943-1991* (1992) [5.144]. Tranfaglia's insightful introduction charts the passive attitudes of successive governments towards the Mafia and the willingness of politicians to establish exchange relationships with it. The breaking of the code of secrecy (*omertà*) by former mafiosi has led to extensive new revelations about the operation of the Mafia. A good deal of the material has now appeared in book form. Tim Shawcroft and Martin Young, *Men of Honour. The Confessions of Tommaso Buscetta* (1987) [5.143] details the revelations of the most important mafioso to date. Pino Arlacchi, *Gli uomini del disonore: la Mafia siciliana nella vita del grande pentito Antonio Calderone* (1992) [5.123] takes the form of a conversation with the *pentito* Antonio Calderone.

Those who have been involved in the front line of the fight against the Mafia have also been more willing than previously to commit their thoughts to page. The most significant example of this is Giovanni Falcone and Marcelle Padovani, *Cose di Cosa Nostra* (1991) [5.131]. Falcone was the leading anti-Mafia crusader of the early 1990s who was killed by a Mafia bomb in broad daylight after his continual requests (in vain) to Rome for greater resources and powers. Public indignation against government ambivalence reached a peak, and the incident set in motion a new government campaign to stamp out the Mafia. Alexander Stille, *Excellent Cadavers: the Mafia and the Death of the First Italian Republic* (1995) [5.145] analyses the most recent period of the Mafia, from 1991 to 1994, documenting the strategic changes in Mafia thinking to preserve their power base in a volatile political situation. The story is a rivetting but familiar one.

The Mafia is, of course, only part of a veritable underworld in Italian society, much of which has been gradually uncovered in the past decade, and has generated a considerable amount of literature. The issues include the secret masonic lodge P2 (*Propaganda Due*), the 'stay-behind' force *Gladio*, the collusion of the security forces and some politicians with fascist terrorist groups, financial scandals involving the Vatican on a massive scale, and the questionable involvement of the United States in the so-called 'secret history' of the Republic. Licio Gelli, Michele Sindona, Roberto Calvi, Archbishop Marcinkus are just some of the names which have excited journalists and others into investigating this underworld. Much of what has been produced is, perhaps inevitably, highly speculative and lacking in the insights which come with solid empirical research. Nevertheless, there are a few books which provide a sufficient comprehension of this underworld and the conspiracy culture with which Italians have become associated.

The broadest overviews are provided by Giorgio Galli, *L'Italia sotterranea: Storia, politica e scandali* (1983) [5.133] and Gianni Cipriani, *I mandanti. Il patto strategico tra massoneria, mafia e poteri politici* (1994) [5.128], the latter of which is a good history from the days of Aldo Moro until the exposure of corruption in the 1990s. The best book, however, is Claudio Gatti, *Rimanga tra noi. L'America, l'Italia, la "questione comunista": i segreti di 50 anni di storia* (1990) [5.135], the particular focus of which is the role of the United States in Italy's postwar history. The book is based on a considerable amount of primary documentation obtained from the American State Department and the CIA itself, as well as on interviews with several people including former CIA agents, Pentagon officials and State Department officials. It will enlighten all those who remain skeptical about the claim that Italy's postwar history cannot be told comprehensively without access to much of what has remained invisible to the public eye. Philip Willan, *Puppet Masters: The Political Use of Terrorism in Italy* [5.147] provides a good account of the manipulation of left wing terrorism by the security services and, ultimately, by the CIA. Although tending towards speculation and ultimately obscure on the role of the United States, the book provides sufficient evidence to justify further research in the area and is the best guide to the Italian underworld for English readers.

The stay-behind-force *Gladio* figures in most of these works, but is tackled in more detail by Antonio Cipriani and Gianni Cipriani, *Storia dell'eversione atlantica in Italia* (1991) [5.127]. The role of the secret masonic lodge P2 (*Propaganda Due*) headed by Licio Gelli, is analysed in Marco Ramat et al., *La resistibile ascesa della P2* (1983) [5.139] and Alberto Cecchi, *Storia della P2* (1985) [5.126]. However, Italian specialists are urged to read the report produced by the parliamentary commission set up to investigate P2: Tina Anselmi, *Relazione della commissione parlamentare d'inchiesta sulla loggia massonica P2* (1984) [5.121] (Anselmi chaired the commission). For an exhaustive history of masonry in Italy, Aldo A. Mola, *Storia della massoneria italiana dalle origini ai nostri giorni* (1993) [5.138] is to be recommended.

The financial scandal involving, amongst others, Roberto Calvi, Michele Sindona and Archbishop Marcinkus (head of the Vatican bank) is analysed in Charles Raw, *The Moneychangers* (1993) [5.140]. It is also investigated in two books focusing on the roles of the two principal characters, Sindona and Calvi. Luigi Di Fonzo, *St. Peter's Banker: Michele Sindona* (1983) [5.130] recounts the role played by Michele Sindona, who died in an American prison through cyanide poisoning (it was never concluded whether it was suicide or murder). The former Italian correspondent for the *Financial Times*, Rupert Cornwell, unravels the financial chicanery and manipulation which led to the death of Roberto Calvi (he was found hanging from Blackfriars Bridge in London), in *God's Banker. An Account of the Life and Death of Roberto Calvi* (1983) [5.129]. The literature already cited in the section on clientelism and corruption in Chapter 2 and on the security services in Chapter 3 is obviously relevant to this section.

NOTES

1. Russell King has also produced a good guide to some of the literature in this wide-ranging area: 'Emigration', in John Loughlin (ed), *Southern European Studies Guide* (London: Bowker-Saur, 1993). Parts of this section draw on King's chapter.

Part Two

ANNOTATED BIBLIOGRAPHY

1
History

GENERAL WORKS

1.1   Castronovo, Valerio. *La storia economica d'Italia*. Torino: Einaudi, 1975.
A comprehensive economic history of Italy, although the text only covers the period until the beginning of the 1970s.

1.2   Clark, Martin. *Modern Italy 1871-1982*. London: Longman, 1984.
The best history of Italy since unification in English. It ranks alongside Mack Smith's [1:13] and is more up to date.

1.3   *Compact storia d'Italia, Cronologia 1815-1990*. Novara: Istituto Geografico de Agostini, 1991.
A condensed chronology of events from 1815 until 1990, including more detailed treatment of selected themes for each year. A useful resource for specialists and excellent summary for beginners.

1.4   Coppa, Frank J. Editor-in-Chief. *Dictionary of Modern Italian History*. Westport: Greenwood Press, 1985.
A useful tool for the beginner and specialist alike, the dictionary covers the main institutions and events in contemporary Italian history.

1.5   Di Scala, Spencer M. *Italy. From Revolution to Republic*. Oxford: Westview Press, 1995.
History of Italy from the eighteenth century to the present.

1.6   Duggan, Christopher. *A Concise History of Italy*. Cambridge: Cambridge University Press, 1994.
A useful introductory history.

1.7   Ginsborg, Paul. *A History of Contemporary Italy*. London: Penguin, 1990.
The best postwar history of Italy in English. It combines social, political and economic analysis in a stimulating and readable manner. One of its major themes is the failure of the Italian state to achieve significant reform. Will need significant updating to account for the dramatic changes in Italian politics in the 1990s.

1.8   Hearder, Harry. *Italy. A Short History*. Cambridge: Cambridge University Press, 1990.
       A brief history of Italy from the classic era to the current period. Ideal for the beginner.

1.9   Kogan, Norman *A Political History of Post War Italy: from the Old to the New Centre-Left*. New York: Praeger, 1981.
       A basic political history of postwar Italy suitable for beginners. Its coverage of events is rather selective.

1.10   Lanaro, Silvio. *Storia Dell'Italia Repubblicana: Dalla Fine Della Guerra agli Anni Novanta*. Venezia: Marsilio, 1992.
       A postwar history of Italy which is particularly good on social, economic and cultural changes.

1.11   Lepre, Aurelio. *Storia della Prima Repubblica: L'Italia dal 1942 al 1992*. Bologna: Mulino, 1993.
       If it is true that the 'First Republic' finished in 1992, this is the only book which provides a complete history of it.

1.12   Levi, Fabio. Levra, Umberto. Tranfaglia, Nicola. Editors. *Il Mondo Contemporaneo. Storia D'Italia*. Firenze: La Nuova Italia, 1978. 3 Vols.
       A useful resource for students pursuing particular themes in Italian history. A different specialist for each chapter outlines the historiography of a specific theme and provides a select bibliography.

1.13   Mack Smith, Dennis. *Italy: A Modern History*. Ann Arbor: University of Michigan Press, 1969.
       For a long time the best history of Italy since unification in English. It is now matched by Clark's more up to date work [1.2].

1.14   Mammarella, Giuseppe. *L'Italia contemporanea (1943-1985)*. Bologna: Mulino, 1986.
       A political history of postwar Italy which analyses successive events in considerable detail.

1.15   Procacci, Giuliano. *History of the Italian People*. London: Penguin, 1991.
       Originally published in France in 1968, this English translation by Anthony Paul is the most widely-read history of the Italian people from their beginnings until the second world war.

1.16   Ruggiero, Romano. Editor. *Storia D'Italia: Annali*. Torino: Einaudi, 1978-.
       This history analyses several concepts and themes rather than adopting a purely chronological analysis.

1.17   Scoppola, Pietro. *La Repubblica dei partiti: profilo storico della democrazia in Italia, 1945-1990*. Bologna: Mulino, 1991.
       This history of postwar Italy has, as its title suggests, a particular emphasis on the important role of the political parties. It is written by a reformist Christian Democrat who played an important role in Italy's political changes of the early 1990s.

SECOND WORLD WAR

1.18   Absalom, Roger. *A Strange Alliance: Aspects of Escape and Survival in Italy 1943-1945*. Firenze: Olschki editore, 1991.
Using a new archival resource (reports of the Allied Screening Commission), this book analyses the nature of the rural world and the role of the peasantry in assisting allied forces after the Armistice.

1.19   Battaglia, R. *Storia della Resistenza italiana*. Torino: Einaudi, 1974, 3rd. edition.
Originally published in 1953, this is a good history of the Resistance movement although perhaps too infused with heroism.

1.20   Colarizzi, Simona. *La seconda guerra mondiale e la Repubblica*. Torino: Utet, 1984.
Volume XXIII of Utet's *Storia d'Italia* (under the general editorship of Giuseppe Galasso) is on Italy and the Second World War.

1.21   Delzell, Charles F. *Mussolini's Enemies: The Italian Anti-Fascist Resistance*. New York: Howard Fertig, 1974, revised edition.
The only complete history in English of the Resistance movement.

1.22   Lamb, Richard. *War in Italy 1943-1945. A Brutal Story*. London: John Murray, 1993.
History of the events from the fall of Mussolini until the final victory, based on previously unused archival material.

1.23   Pavone, Claudio. *Una guerra civile: saggio storico sulla moralità nella resistenza*. Torino: Bollati Boringhieri, 1991.
A path breaking study of the Resistance movement. A product of twenty years of research and a wealth of primary source material, it is the only work to use the perspective of the participants themselves to explore the internal nature of the movement.

1.24   Quazza, Guido. *Resistenza e Storia d'Italia: problemi e ipotesi di ricerca*. Milano: Feltrinelli, 1976.
The standard account of the Resistance until the publication of Pavone's work [1.23].

1.25   Tosi, F. F. Grassi, G. Legnani, Massimo. Editors. *L'Italia nella seconda guerra mondiale e nella Resistenza* Milano: Feltrinelli, 1988.
The best overall account of Italy's role in the Second World War and the Resistance movement.

POSTWAR SETTLEMENT

1.26   AA.VV (Various Authors). *Italia 1945-48. Le origini della Repubblica*. Torino: G. Giuppichelli, 1974.
One of the best multi-authored collections available on the postwar settlement.

1.27   AA.VV (Various Authors). *La società italiana dalla Resistenza alla guerra fredda*. Milano: Teti, 1989.
       Volume 23 of Teti's multi-authored *Storia della società italiana* focuses on the Resistance and the postwar settlement.

1.28   Branca, G. Editor. *Commenatario della costituzione*. Bologna: Zanichelli & Il Foro Italiano, 1975-.
       Still in course of publication, this is the most comprehensive analysis of the Italian constitution.

1.29   Calamandrei, Piero. Levi, P. *Commentario sistematico alla costituzione italiana*. Firenze: Edizione lavoro, 1950
       Although dated, one of the best commentaries to be found on the Italian constitution.

1.30   Daneo, Carlo. *La politica economica della ricostruzione 1945-49*. Torino: Einaudi, 1975.
       An account of the economic reconstruction of Italy in the immediate postwar period.

1.31   De Felice, Renzo. Editor. *Resistenza e Repubblica, 1943-1956*. Roma: Lucarini, 1985.
       Volume 5 of *Storia dell'Italia contemporanea* is on the period from the Resistance until 1956.

1.32   Ellwood, David W. *Italy, 1943-1945*. Leicester: Leicester University Press, 1985.
       The most readable account in English of the end of the war and the beginnings of reconstruction.

1.33   Falzone, V. Palermo, F. Consentino, F. Editors. *La Costituzione della Repubblica italiana: illustrata con i lavori preparatori e corredata da note e riferimenti*. Milano: Mondadori, 1976.
       One of the best collections on the Italian constitution, it shows how the various articles came to be drafted in the way they were.

1.34   Gallerano, Nicola. Editor. *L'altro dopoguerra. Roma e il Sud 1943-45*. Milano: Angeli, 1985.
       An analysis of the South of Italy in the two critical years 1943-45 at the end of the war.

1.35   Harper, John Lamberton. *America and the Reconstruction of Italy, 1945-48*. Cambridge: Cambridge University Press, 1986.
       A good analysis of the role played by the United States in the reconstruction period.

1.36   Istituto nazionale per la storia del movimento di Liberazione in Italia. Editor. *L'Italia dalla Liberazione alla Repubblica*. Milano: Feltrinelli, 1977.
       A good multi-authored account of the Italian postwar settlement, edited by the Italian National Institute of the History of the Liberation Movement.

1.37   Legnani, Massimo. Editor. *L'Italia dal 1943 al 1948. Lotte politiche e sociali.*
       Torino: Loescher, 1973.
       One of the best collections in Italian on the political, social and economic
       conditions during the postwar settlement.

1.38   Levi, Fabio. Rugafiori, Paride. Vento, S. *Il triangolo industriale tra ricostruzione
       e lotta di classe, 1945-1948.* Milano: Feltrinelli, 1974.
       An account of the industrial North and working class militancy during
       reconstruction.

1.39   Manzocchi, Bruzio. *Lineamenti di politica economica in Italia (1945-1948).*
       Roma: Editori Riuniti, 1960.
       An analysis of the competing economic alternatives at the end of the war and the
       economic policies which prevailed.

1.40   Miller, James Edward. *The United States and Italy, 1940-1950.* Chapel Hill: The
       University of North Carolina Press, 1986.
       A broad overview of Italo-American relations in the war and during the
       reconstruction period.

1.41   Peaslee, Amos J. *The Constitutions of Nations.* The Hague: Nijhoff, 1965-70,
       3rd. edition.
       Complete editions of the Italian constitution in English are hard to find. Volume
       2 of this work contains the full text in English.

1.42   Quartararo, R. *Italia e Stati Uniti. Gli anni difficili (1945-1952).* Napoli: Edizioni
       Scientifiche Italiane, 1986.
       One of the best accounts in Italian of relations between the United States and Italy
       in the immediate postwar period.

1.43   Salvati, Mariuccia. *Stato e industria nella ricostruzione. Alle origini del potere
       democristiano 1944/1949.* Milano: Feltrinelli, 1982.
       A good historical analysis of Italian political economy. By focusing on the state
       and economic reconstruction, Salvati shows how the Christian Democrats began
       building a power base for themselves from early on in the postwar period.

1.44   Smith, Timothy. *The United States, Italy and NATO 1947-1952.* London:
       Macmillan, 1991.
       An analysis of Italy and its international environment during the critical years
       when NATO was founded.

1.45   Terracini, Umberto. *Come nacque la Costituzione.* Roma: Editori Riuniti, 1978.
       Terracini was a Communist and member of the Constituent Assembly. His
       account of the origins of the Italian constitution, although coloured by his own
       political standpoint, offers a clear outline to the constitutional debates, the
       conflicts and how they were resolved.

1.46   Tobagi, Walter. *La rivoluzione impossibile: l'attentato a Togliatti - violenza
       politica e reazione popolare.* Milano: Il Saggiatore, 1978.
       A rivetting account of the assassination attempt on the leader of the Italian
       Communist Party, Palmiro Togliatti, and the attempt by many communists to use

this opportunity to provoke an insurrection, something stopped by instructions from Togliatti himself from his hospital bed.

1.47   Woolf, Stuart. Editor. *The Rebirth of Italy 1943-1950*. London: Longman, 1972. The best collection in English on the postwar settlement. The concluding chapter by the editor provides an excellent overview of the period.

1950s-1960s

1.48   AA.VV (Various Authors). *Il miracolo economico e il centro-sinistra*. Milano: Teti, 1990.
Vol. 24 of Teti's multi-authored *Storia della società italiana* covers the 1950s and 1960s (the economic miracle and the centre-left experiment).

1.49   Bocca, Giorgio. *Miracolo all'italiano*. Milano: Feltrinelli, 1980.
An account of Italy's so-called 'economic miracle' of the 1950s and early 1960s.

1.50   Duggan, Christopher. Wagstaffe, Christopher. Editors. *Italy in the Cold War. Politics, Culture and Society, 1948-1958*. Oxford: Berg, 1995.
The only book available which is specifically focused on Italy in the Cold War. Includes an assessment of its impact on intellectual and cultural life.

1.51   King, Russell. *Land Reform: The Italian Experience*. London: Butterworth, 1973.
The only text in English to deal in detail with Italy's important agrarian reform of the 1950s.

1.52   LaPalombara, Joseph. *Italy: The Politics of Planning*. Syracuse, New York: Syracuse University Press, 1966.
Charts the rise and fall of the Italian planning experiment of the 1950s and 1960s.

1.53   Murgia, Piergiuseppe. *Il luglio 1960*. Milano: Feltrinelli, 1960.
A study of the short-lived Tambroni government of 1960, which marked a watershed in Italian government, confirming that fascist-supported governments were not tenable.

1.54   Parlato, Valentino. Editor. *Spazio e ruolo del riformismo*. Bologna: Mulino, 1974.
A good synthesis of the debate about the controversial centre-left experiment in the 1960s.

1.55   Scalfari, Eugenio. *Rapporto sul neo-capitalismo in Italia*. Bari: Laterza, 1961.
An evaluation of the significance of the economic achievements of the 1950s and their political implications.

1.56   Tarrow, Sidney. *Peasant Communism in Southern Italy*. New Haven: Yale University Press, 1967.
An excellent study of southern politics in the 1950s, it explains the failure of the Communists and the roots of Christian Democratic power in the south. It also highlights, via an analysis of parties, the differences existing between the Italian North and South.

1.57   Tamburrano, Giuseppe. *Storia e cronaca della centro-sinstra*. Milano: Feltrinelli, 1971.
Provides the most detailed chronological account of the rise and fall of the centre-left coalitional experiment in the 1960s.

1970s-1990s

1.58   AA.VV (Various Authors). *Nuovi equilibri e nuove prospettivi*. Milano: Teti Editore, 1990.
Vol. 25 of Teti's *Storia della società italiana* is focused on the 1970s and contains a wide range of chapters by specialists in their fields.

1.59   Baldissera, A. *La rivolta dei quarantamila: dai quadri FIAT ai COBAS*. Milano: Feltrinelli, 1980.
An analysis of grassroots worker militancy in the watershed year of 1980 (the Fiat strike) and beyond.

1.60   Benzoni, Alberto. Gritti, Roberto. *La terra di nessuno. Alla ricerca della Repubblica perduta*. Firenze: Origami Edizioni lavoro, 1995.
An analysis of the political crisis of the 1990s including reference to the ill-fated Berlusconi government of 1994. Benzoni is an ex-member of the socialist party.

1.61   Bocca, Giorgio. *Moro: una tragedia italiana*. Milano: Bompiani, 1978.
There is a wealth of literature on the Moro kidnapping. This book includes most of Moro's prison letters which the Christian Democratic party always claimed were not written by him. The book also includes a chronology of events by Silvia Giacomoni.

1.62   Braun, Michael. *L'Italia da Andreotti a Berlusconi. Rivolgimenti e prospettive politiche in un paese a rischio*. Milano: Feltrinelli, 1995.
A useful historical account of the origins and course of the crisis of the 1990s.

1.63   Brunetta, Renato. *Il modello Italia. Analisi e chronache degli anni ottanta*. Venezia: Marsilio, 1991.
A good analysis of Italy's economy and society in the 1980s. The Italian 'model' is described through a number of anomalies and disparities in growth and development.

1.64   Caciagli, Mario. Cazzola, Franco. Morlino, Leonardo. Passigli, Stefano. Editors. *L'Italia fra crisi e transizione*. Bari: Laterza, 1994.
Thus far the best book produced on the changes which the Italian political system is undergoing in the 1990s, including contributions from key specialists: Barnes, Calise, Cartocci, Cheli, Cotta, LaPalombara, Mastropaolo, Morisi, Pasquino, Predieri, Regonini, Zannotti.

1.65   Cafagna, Luciano. *La grande slavina. L'Italia verso la crisi*. Venezia: Marsilio, 1993.
One of the better analyses of the crisis of the early 1990s.

1.66   Calise, Mauro. *Dopo la partitocrazia. L'Italia tra modelli e realtà*. Torino:
        Einaudi, 1995.
        Captures well the problems of the Italian political system in the mid-1990s.

1.67   Cavazza, Fabio Luca. Graubard, Stephen R. Editors. *Il caso italiano. Italia
        anni'70*. Milan: Garzanti, 1975, 2 volumes.
        Focused on the so-called anomalies of the Italian political system in the 1970s,
        and comparable with the Graziano/Tarrow volume [1:73].

1.68   Cavazza, Fabio Luca. Editor. *La riconquista dell'Italia. Economia. Istituzioni.
        Politica*. Milano: Longanesi, 1993.
        Of wide ranging subject matter (and including a large number of contributors) this
        is designed as a follow-up to the earlier Cavazza/Graubard volume [1:67]. The
        book argues that the anomalies of the Italian case are fading and 'normality' is
        being won.

1.69   De Lalla Millal, Paolo. *Topografia politica della Seconda Repubblica. 1. La
        destra*. Napoli: Edizioni Scientifiche Italiane, 1994.
        First of a series of books on the collapse of the so-called 'old order' and the rise
        of new political forces, this volume is focused on the rise of the right.

1.70   Foa, Vittorio. Ginsborg, Paul. Et al. *Le virtù della Repubblica. Dalla crisi del
        sistema e dal ricambio della classe politica lo spazio per una nuova cultura di
        governo*. Milano: Il Saggiatore, 1994.
        Transcript of a discussion that took place at the end of 1993 between a group of
        well known observers of the Italian political scene. Stimulating and enlightening
        observations on the past, present and likely future of the Italian Republic.

1.71   Gilbert, Mark. *The Italian Revolution. The Ignominous End of Politics, Italian
        Style*. Oxford: Westview, 1995.
        Account of the dramatic changes in Italian politics in the late 1980s and early
        1990s.

1.72   Ginsborg, Paul. Editor. *Stato dell'Italia*. Milano: Il Saggiatore Mondadori, 1994.
        The most comprehensive survey of Italy in the 1980s and 1990s found in one
        volume. Brings together 130 contributors with over 180 separate articles and 700
        pages, including 90 pages of statistics. Covers politics, institutions, society,
        culture and economic development, and is accessible to non-academics.

1.73   Graziano, Luigi. Tarrow, Sidney. Editors. *La crisi italiana*. Torino: Einaudi,
        1979, 2 vols.
        A collection of considerable significance on the economic and political problems
        of the 1970s. Several of the pieces have become standard reference points for
        many authors. Should be seen in conjunction with the Cavazza/Graubard volume
        [1:67].

1.74   Gundle, Stephen. Parker, Simon. Editors. *The New Italian Republic. From the
        Fall of Communism to the Rise of Berlusconi*. London: Routledge, 1995.
        The best book in English on the dramatic changes in Italian politics in the early
        1990s. Also includes chapters on the old regime.

1.75   Lombardo, Antonio. Editor. *Il sistema disintegrato. Il sistema politico italiano tra sviluppo e crisi (1974-77)*. Milano: SugarCo, 1977.
Focuses on the critical years of the so-called Historic Compromise, when minority governments survived through the abstention of the communists in parliament. The failed experiment proved to be a watershed in the development of the Italian political system.

1.76   Lupi, Giancarlo. *Il crollo della grande coalizione: la strategia delle elites dei partiti (1976-1979)*. Milano: SugarCo, 1982.
Analyses the strategies of the various parties during the period of the so-called Historic Compromise, 1976-1979.

1.77   Salvadori, Massimo L. *Storia d'Italia e crisi di un regime: alle radici della politica italiana*. Bologna: Mulino, 1994.
A short historical profile of Italy from 1860 onwards written from the perspective of an Italian anomaly: the failure of successive regimes to achieve alternation in government. Locates the crisis of the early 1990s in a useful historical perspective.

1.78   Scarano, Mimmo. De Luca, Maurizio. *Il mandarino è marcio. Terrorismo e cospirazione nel caso Moro*. Roma: Editori Riuniti, 1985.
One of the better accounts of the Moro kidnapping, the book attempts to unravel the role played by the Italian and foreign (and particularly American) security services.

1.79   Teodori, Massimo. *Una nuova Repubblica? Il voto e la riforma elettorale, il tramonto dei partiti, la questione del governo nella democrazia dell'alternanza*. Milano: Sperling & Kupfer, 1994.
General analysis of the deep changes in Italian politics of the early 1990s. Evaluates whether the changes constitute the birth of a 'new republic.'

1.80   Turani, Giuseppe. *1985-1995. Il secondo miracolo economico italiano: istruzioni per l'uso*. Milano: Sperling & Kupfer, 1986.
Although rather premature in its prognosis and prescriptions (it fails to predict the economic downturn of the early 1990s), this is nonetheless a useful account of the turnaround in the Italian economy achieved in the 1980s, after the problems besetting it in the 1970s.

1.81   Wagner-Pacifici, Robin Erica. *The Moro Morality Play. Terrorism as Social Drama*. Chicago: University of Chicago Press, 1986.
An unusual but readable book, adopting a dramaturgic approach to the Moro kidnapping.

BIOGRAPHIES, MEMOIRS, SPEECHES, WRITINGS

1.82   Andreotti, Giulio. *Intervista su De Gasperi*. Bari: Laterza, 1977.
The most prevalent politician of the Italian Republic (seven-times Prime Minister Andreotti) being interviewed about the politician most associated with the postwar settlement and the early success of the Christian Democrats, Alcide De Gasperi.

He was leader of the party 1945-46 and eight times Prime Minister between 1945 and 1953.

1.83   Bocca, Giorgio. *Palmiro Togliatti*. Bari: Laterza, 1977.
A good biography of the postwar leader of the Italian Communist Party (PCI) by one of Italy's leading writers and journalists. Togliatti was responsible for relaunching the PCI in the postwar period as a modern mass party.

1.84   Carli, Guido. *Intervista sul capitalismo italiano*. Bari: Laterza, 1977.
A book-length interview with the ex-Governor of the Bank of Italy about the state of the Italian economy in the 1970s.

1.85   Colombo, Furio. *In Italy. Post War Political Life: interviews with Andreotti, Nenni, Terracini, Spriano, La Malfa, Lama, Saraceno, Carli*. New York: Karz Publishers, 1981.
One of the few books in English which interviews top politicians and other leading figures in Italian political and economic life.

1.86   Coppola, Aniellio. *Moro*. Milano: Feltrinelli, 1976.
One of the best biographies of the ex-leader of the Christian Democrats who was kidnapped and then murdered by the Red Brigades in 1978.

1.87   De Gasperi, Maria Romana. Editor. *De Gasperi scrive. Corrispondenza con capi di stato, cardinali, uomini politici giornalisti, diplomatici*. Brescia: Morcelliana, 1974, 2 vols.
A selection of Alcide De Gasperi's correspondence and writings.

1.88   Di Nicola, Primo. *Mario Segni*. Milano: Sperling & Kupfer, 1992.
An account of the political life of the reformist Christian Democrat, Mario Segni, who was responsible for pushing forward the reform movement in the early 1990s and who eventually left the party in 1993 to set up his own political movement which failed to fulfil expectations.

1.89   *Dizionario biografico degli italiani*. Roma: Istituto della Enciclopedia italiana, 1960-.
A multi-volumed encyclopaedia providing short descriptions of all significant figures in Italian life.

1.90   Foa, Vittorio. *Il cavallo e la torre. Riflessioni su una vita*. Torino: Einaudi, 1991.
The autobiography of the influential ex-leader of the CGIL (communist-socialist trade union) and a major figure in left wing politics generally.

1.91   Galli, Giorgio. *Fanfani*. Milano: Feltrinelli, 1975.
A good biography of one of the key Christian Democratic figures of postwar politics. Fanfani was responsible for starting the process of changing the Christian Democrats into a modern mass party in the 1950s.

1.92   Giolitti, Antonio. *Lettere a Marta: ricordi e riflessioni*. Bologna: Mulino, 1992.
The diaries of a communist party member who left the party in the watershed year 1956 (Kruschev's revelations about Stalin and the Soviet invasion of Hungary) to

become a socialist and minister in the first centre-left government in the early 1960s.

1.93   Gramsci, Antonio. *Opere*. Torino: Einaudi, 1970-, 12 volumes.
The complete works of Gramsci, the founder and first leader of the Italian Communist Party and arguably the most original Marxist theorist of the twentieth century. He died in a Fascist prison in the 1930s.

1.94   La Malfa, Ugo. (Edited by Giancarlo Tartaglia). *Scritti 1925-1953*. Milano: Mondadori, 1988.
The political writings of the ex-leader of the Republican Party, and one of the most respected of postwar Italian politicians. Contains incisive comment on the reconstruction period. A second volume is due to appear.

1.95   Lama, Luciano. *Intervista sul sindacato*. Bari: Laterza, 1976.
A book length interview with the ex-leader of the CGIL (communist socialist trade union) and active communist (to the right of the party) in a period when trade union power in Italy was probably at its peak.

1.96   Lombardi, Riccardo. (Edited by Simona Colarizzi). *Scritti politici, 1945-1978*. Venezia: Marsilio, 1978, 2 vols.
Political writings of the former leader of the Italian Socialist Party.

1.97   Lorusso, Mino. *Occhetto. Il comunismo italiano da Togliatti al PDS*. Firenze: Ponte alle Grazie, 1992.
The best biography available on the ex-leader of the Italian Communist Party and the man responsible for its social democratisation. Lorusso's work is critical in approach and argues that, contrary to the conventional wisdom, Occhetto had never been on the left of the party and that his actions in the late 1980s were therefore unsurprising.

1.98   Mafai, Miriam. *L'uomo che sognava la lotta armata*. Milano: Rizzoli, 1984.
A good biography of Pietro Secchia, the leading member of the more orthodox faction of the Italian Communist Party in the 1950s and probably the last member of the party who seriously considered armed revolution as a viable prospect. For a short period of time, he was a possible alternative to Togliatti for the leadership of the party, and the book explains much about the ambiguities of postwar Italian communism.

1.99   Moro, Aldo. *L'intelligenza e gli avvenimenti. Testi 1959-1978*. Milano: Garzanti: 1979.
A collection of Aldo Moro's writings between 1959 and 1978. Moro was leader of the Christian Democratic leader and Prime Minister and was kidnapped and murdered by the Red Brigades in 1978.

1.100   Nenni, Pietro. *Intervista sul socialismo italiano*. Bari: Laterza, 1977.
A book-length interview with the leader of the Italian Socialist Party in the immediate postwar period.

1.101   Nenni, Pietro. *Diari*. Milano: SugarCo Edizioni, 3 volumes: *Tempo di Guerra Fredda. Diari 1943-1956* (1981); *Gli anni del centrosinistra. Diari 1957-1966* (1982); *I conti con la storia. Diari 1967-1971* (1983).
One of the few Italian politicians to keep a reasonably comprehensive diary. Nenni was leader of the Socialist Party and the diaries contain some unique insights into the nature of postwar politics in Italy.

1.102   Pallotta, Gino. *Andreotti, il Richelieu della politica italiana*. Roma: Newton Compton, 1988.
One of the best biographies of Giulio Androtti, who had the longest political career in Italy. Published a couple of years too early to include Andreotti's downfall under accusations of collusion with the mafia.

1.103   Parri, Ferrucio. (Edited by E. Collotti, G. Rochat, G. Solaro Pelazza, R. Speziale). *Scritti 1915/1975*. Milano: Feltrinelli, 1976.
The writings of the leader of the short-lived Action Party. Parri was briefly Prime Minister during the postwar settlement, and the fall of his government was viewed as a general failure of progressive political forces to exploit the power vacuum to their benefit.

1.104   Rumor, Mariano. (Edited by E. Reato and F. Malgeri). *Memorie (1943-1970)*. Vincenza: Pozza, 1991.
Well-written and informative memoirs of Mariano Rumor, leader of the Christian Democratic Party 1964-8, and three-times Prime Minister during one of Italy's more turbulent periods (1968-1970).

1.105   Santarelli, Enzo. *Nenni*. Torino: Utet, 1993.
Biography of Pietro Nenni, the leader of the Italian Socialist Party in the immediate postwar period.

1.106   Saraceno, Pasquale. *Intervista sulla Ricostruzione 1943-1953*. Bari: Laterza, 1977.
Interview with the leading Christian Democrat economist on the postwar settlement and reconstruction of Italy.

1.107   Saragat, Giuseppe. *Quarant'anni di lotta per la democrazia. Scritti e discorsi 1925-1965*. Milano: Mursia, 1966.
Writings and speeches of the former leader of the Italian Social Democratic Party (PSDI) who became President of Italy.

1.108   Scoppola, Pietro. *La proposta politica di De Gasperi*. Bologna: Mulino, 1977.
Interview with one of Italy's leading historians (a Christian Democrat reformist) about the political significance of the first leader of the party and eight-times Prime Minister, Alcide De Gasperi.

1.109   Togliatti, Palmiro. Ragionieri, Ernesto (Editor). Gruppi, Luciano (Editor). *Opere*. Roma: Editori Riuniti, 1973-, 6 volumes.
The complete works of the first and most significant postwar leader of the Italian Communist Party, a theoretician and tactician with an immense influence in the party and Italian politics generally. The last two volumes are not of the quality in production of the first four.

1.110 Valentini, Chiara. *Berlinguer, Il Segretario*. Milano: Mondadori, 1987.
       A good (and largely sympathetic) biography of the leader of the Italian
       Communist Party in the 1970s and 1980s, and the man responsible for
       masterminding the (failed) Historic Compromise with Italian Christian Democracy
       in the mid-1970s.

1.111 Zunino, Pier Giorgio. Editor. *Scritti politici di Alcide De Gasperi*. Milano:
       Feltrinelli, 1979.
       The political writings of Italy's most important political leader of the immediate
       postwar period, with an introduction by the editor. De Gasperi was leader of the
       Christian Democratic Party 1945-46 and eight-times Prime Minister between 1945
       and 1953.

2

Politics

GENERAL WORKS

2.1 (Various Editors). *Italian Politics: A Review.* London: Pinter, 1986-1993.
A yearbook which is an important source of material on current Italian politics. There are different editors each year (or each pair of years), and the themes vary according to the prominence of different issues in the year in question. Simultaneous appearance in Italian and published by Mulino [2.2]. Pinter, from 1994, ceased publishing it, and there now appear to be two versions of the yearbook, one by Avebury under the original English title (but no volumes have been published as yet) and one by Westview Press, the first volume of which is Gianfranco Pasquino and Carol Mershon (eds), *Italian Politics. Ending the First Republic* (1994). Despite the different title, Westview maintain the agreement with Mulino to publish an Italian version each year (although Avebury may have established an agreement with an alternative Italian publisher).

2.2 (Various Editors). *Politica in Italia. I fatti dell'anno e le interpretazioni.* Bologna: Mulino: 1986-.
Italian version of [2.1].

2.3 Adams, John Clarke. Barile, Paolo. *The Government of Republican Italy.* Boston: Houghton Mifflin, 1972.
One of the earliest text books in English, it has a basic legalistic orientation.

2.4 Allum, Percy. *Italy — Republic Without Government.* London: Weidenfeld and Nicolson, 1973.
The first substantial political science textbook on Italy written by a British Italianist. It still has much to commend it as an analysis of Italian politics in the 1950s and 1960s.

2.5 Bevilacqua, Piero. Carboni, Carlo. Levi, Fabio. Lupo, Salvatore. Mangiameli, Rosario. Pavone, Claudio. Tranfaglia, Nicola. Triglia, Carlo. *Lezioni sull'Italia repubblicana.* Roma: Donzelli, 1994.
Collection evaluating the experience of the Italian Republic from a number of chronological and thematic perspectives. The contributors are all well-known specialists in various fields.

2.6   Bobbio, Norberto. *Saggi sulla scienza politica in Italia.* Bari: Laterza, 1977, 2nd. edition.
       Originally published in 1971, a collection of key writings on Italian political science by one of Italy's most famous contemporary theorists.

2.7   Bocca, Giorgio. *La disunità d'Italia.* Milano: Garzanti, 1990.
       Penetrating journalistic analysis of the Italian political scene in 1990.

2.8   Bull, Martin J. Rhodes, Martin. Editors. *Transition and Crisis in Italian Politics.* London: Cass, 1996.
       A special issue of *West European Politics,* this collection brings together several specialists to analyse the changes in Italian politics and government during the 1980s and 1990s. It can be regarded as a form of generational follow-up to [2.23].

2.9   Ciuffoletti, Zeffiro. Noiret, Serge. Editors. *I modelli di democrazia in Europa e il caso italiano.* Firenze: Ponte alle Grazie, 1992.
       An introductory book which describes Italian politics in comparative context.

2.10   Donovan, Mark. Editor. *Italy.* Aldershot: Dartmouth Press, 1996.
       Part of the publisher's series 'The International Library of Politics and Comparative Government', this is a collection of approximately twenty-five key journal articles on Italy, usefully organised into several sections recognisable to students of politics and government.

2.11   Farneti, Paolo. *Il sistema politico italiano.* Bologna: Mulino, 1973.
       The first substantial political science text book on Italy, regarded as seminal by many because of the subsequent studies it stimulated.

2.12   Graziano, Luigi. Editor. *La scienza politica in Italia: bilancio e prospettive* Milan: Franco Angeli, 1986.
       A thematic guide to Italian political science. A specialist for each chapter provides a historiography of a specific theme and a useful bibliography.

2.13   Hine, David. *Governing Italy. The Politics of Bargained Pluralism.* Oxford: Oxford University Press, 1992.
       A solid, largely conventional textbook with a main focus on institutions.

2.14   Kesselman, Mark. Et al. *European Politics in Transition.* Toronto: D.C. Heath, 1992.
       Originally published in 1987, the substantial section on Italy by Stephen Hellman provides a good introduction to Italian politics and government.

2.15   Koole, Ruud A. Mair, Peter. Editors. *Political Data Yearbook.* London: Sage, 1992-.
       Begun in 1992 and published in association with the *European Journal of Political Research* this venture outlines developments in European politics in the previous year, and includes a chapter on Italy. An overview of the year's political developments is accompanied by data on the composition of the governing coalition(s) and other relevant matters. The first few issues suggest that this will become an indispensable resource for researchers.

2.16   LaPalombara, Joseph. *Democracy Italian Style*. New Haven: Yale University Press, 1979.
Controversial and lively, this book takes revisionism of the old 'subcultural' model to the extreme in redefining postwar Italy as an example of stable democracy.

2.17   Morlino, Leonardo. Editor. *Scienza Politica*. Torino: Edizioni della Fondazione Giovanni Agnelli, 1989.
A general guide to political science with a natural emphasis on Italy.

2.18   Pallotta, Gino. *Dizionario della politica italiana*. Roma: Newton Compton, 1985.
A useful guide in dictionary form through the maze of Italian politics.

2.19   Pasquino, Gianfranco. Editor. *Il Sistema Politico Italiano*. Rome: Laterza, 1985.
Most of the contributions to this book have already been published elsewhere, but together they constitute an informed analysis of the Italian political system.

2.20   Putnam, Robert. (With Robert Leonardi and Raffaella Nanetti). *Making Democracy Work. Civic Traditions in Modern Italy*. Princeton: Princeton University Press, 1992.
Seminal work on Italy and institutional performance generally. Through a study of Italian regional governments since 1970 the book explains institutional performance in terms of the development of a civic local culture, itself determined by particular patterns of historical development.

2.21   Sassoon, Donald. *Contemporary Italy: Politics, Economy and society Since 1945*. London: Longman, 1986.
A solid, if unconventional, text book which attempts to unravel the relationship between economics, society and politics in postwar Italy.

2.22   Spotts, Frederic. Weiser, Theodor. *Italy: A Difficult Democracy*. Cambridge: Cambridge University Press, 1986.
A conventional text-book which is lively and well-written but lacks academic incisiveness and is bibliographically rather thin.

2.23   Tarrow, Sidney. Lange, Peter. *Italy in Transition. Conflict and Consensus*. London: Frank Cass, 1979.
A milestone in the study of Italian politics, this volume (originally a special issue of *West European Politics*) attempts to use comparative techniques of analysis to study Italy. Still essential reading to understand Italian politics in the period until the 1970s. See [2.8] for special issue of *West European Politics* on the 1980s and 1990s.

2.24   Zariski, Raphael. *Italy: The Politics of Uneven Development*. Hinsdale: Dryden Press, 1972.
The first substantial political science textbook on Italy written by a North American. Its basic theme is that the Italy suffers from 'political lag' compared with its social and economic development. Although some aspects of Italian politics are not given the emphasis which later developments showed they required, the book remains relevant today.

POLITICAL PARTIES AND THE PARTY SYSTEM: GENERAL STUDIES

2.25   Colarizzi, Simona. *Storia dei partiti nell'Italia repubblicana*. Bari: Laterza, 1994.
A large volume, and one of the best general introductions to Italian political parties available. Contains a useful bibliography.

2.26   Corona, Cleofe. Editor. *Il costo della democrazia: i partiti politici italiani, costi e finanziamenti*. Roma: Ispes, 1984.
Proceedings of a conference held in 1983, this is a good source of information on the financing of Italian political parties.

2.27   Farneti, Paolo. *The Italian Party System*. London: Pinter, 1985.
The most comprehensive analysis in English of the Italian party system. Finished by others after Farneti's premature death.

2.28   Galli, Giorgio. Prandi, Alfonso. *Patterns of Political Participation in Italy*. New Haven: Yale University Press, 1970.
A synthesis of a multi-volumed study in Italian, this remains one of the most detailed analyses available in English on Italy's two main postwar political parties, the Christian Democrats and the Communists.

2.29   Galli, Giorgio. *Il bipartitismo imperfetto. Comunisti e democristiani in Italia*. Milano: Mondadori, 1984.
Originally published in the late 1960s, it develops the author's model of Italy's 'imperfect two party system'.

2.30   Galli, Giorgio. *I partiti politici italiani, 1943-1991. Dalla Resistenza all'Europa integrata*. Torino: Utet, 1992.
The most recent edition of the author's well-known history of Italian political parties.

2.31   Katz, Richard. Mair, Peter. Editors. *Party Organizations in Western Democracies 1960-1990*. London: Sage, 1992-1993, 2 vols.
The best source for statistical data on Italian political parties.

2.32   Pacifici, Giorgio. *Il costo della democrazia: i partiti italiani attraverso i loro bilanci*. Roma: Caduno, 1983.
A thorough analysis of the debt-ridden finances of the Italian political parties in the 1970s and 1980s.

2.33   Panebianco, Angelo. *Political Parties: Organisation and Power*. Cambridge: Cambridge University Press, 1988.
Path breaking general study of political parties, where the influence of the author's knowledge of Italian parties is apparent. The quality of the book is testimony to Italian political science's primary focus on the study of political parties.

2.34   Pasquino, Gianfranco. *Degenerazioni e riforme dei partiti*. Bari: Laterza, 1982.
A good analysis of the parties and their saturating control of the state.

2.35   Pridham, Geoffrey. *Political Parties and Coalition Behaviour in Italy*. London:
       Routledge, 1988.
       A comprehensive analysis of Italian coalition behaviour.

2.36   Sartori, Giovanni. *Correnti, frazioni e fazioni nei partiti politici italiani*. Bologna:
       Mulino, 1973.
       An early work on party factionalism, still useful today.

2.37   Sartori, Giovanni. *Parties and Party Systems: A Framework for Analysis*.
       Cambridge: Cambridge University Press, 1976.
       Path breaking contribution to the study of parties and party systems. Contains the
       author's party system typology which includes 'polarised pluralism', extrapolated
       from the Italian case.

2.38   Sartori, Giovanni. *Teoria dei partiti e caso italiano*. Milano: SugarCo, 1982.
       A collection of Sartori's key writings, essential to understanding his theoretical
       model of 'polarised pluralism'.

2.39   Tamburrano, Giuseppe. *Pci e Psi nel sistema democristiano*. Bari: Laterza, 1978.
       Written in the 1970s, this book captures the dilemma and problems of the two
       main parties of the left (Socialists and Communists) in relation to the political
       dominance of the Christian Democrats.

2.40   Vallauri, C. Editor. *I partiti italiani tra declino e riforma*. Roma: Bulzoni
       Editore, 1986.
       One of the last comprehensive guides to Italian political parties published before
       the transformation of the traditional parties and party system in the early 1990s.

POLITICAL PARTIES: INDIVIDUAL STUDIES

Italian Communism (PCI/PDS, PDUP, RC)

2.41   Accornero, Aris. Mannheimer, Renato. and Sebastiani, C. *L'identità comunista,
       i militanti, le strutture, la cultura del PCI*. Rome: Editori Riuniti, 1983.
       The most thorough sociological study of a political party in Italy, it is based on
       a survey of 16,000 delegates to the PCI's provincial congresses in 1979.

2.42   Amyot, Grant. *The Italian Communist Party. The Crisis of the Popular Front
       Strategy*. London: Croom Helm, 1981.
       An analysis of the political divisions inside the PCI in the postwar period, with
       a specific focus on the Amendola-Ingrao dispute of the 1960s.

2.43   Belligni, Silvano. Editor. *La giraffa e il liocorno. Il Pci dagli anni'70 al nuovo
       decennio*. Milano: Franco Angeli, 1983.
       A diverse range of themes is covered in this collection on the PCI in the 1970s.

2.44   Blackmer, Donald. *Unity in Diversity. Italian Communism and the Communist
       World*. Cambridge: MIT Press, 1968.
       One of the best early studies of the Italian Communist Party and its relations with
       the Soviet Union. Superseded by the work of Joan Bath Urban [2:58].

2.45   Blackmer, Donald L. M. Tarrow, Sidney. *Communism in Italy and France.*
       Princeton: Princeton University Press, 1979.
       Originally published in 1975, a milestone in the study of west European
       communism. It refocused attention on the national environments of these parties.
       Essential reading for specialists of Italian communism.

2.46   Femia, Joseph V. *Gramsci's Political Thought: Hegemony, Consciousness and the
       Revolutionary Process.* Oxford: Clarendon Press, 1981.
       Commentary on Gramsci's political thought.

2.47   Garavini, Sergio. *Le ragioni di un comunista. Scritti e riflessioni sullo
       scioglimento del Pci e sulla nascita di una nuova forza comunista in Italia.* Roma:
       Datanews, 1991.
       Reflections of the first leader of *Rifondazione comunista* (RC), the party formed
       from a split in the PCI when it transformed itself into the Democratic Party of the
       Left (PDS).

2.48   Garzia, Aldo. (1985) *Da Natta a Natta. Storia del Manifesto e del PDUP* Bari:
       Dedalo, 1985.
       History of the Manifesto Group and the Democratic Party of Proletarian Unity for
       Communism, both products of a split in the PCI in the late 1960s.

2.49   Gramsci, Antonio. (Hoare, Quinton. Nowell-Smith, Geoffrey. Editors). *Selections
       From the Prison Notebooks.* London: Lawrence & Wishart, 1971.
       The best edition in English of Gramsci's prison writings. Essential reading for any
       historian of the PCI.

2.50   Hellman, Stephen. *Italian Communism in Transition. The Rise and Fall of the
       Historic Compromise in Turin, 1975-1980.* Oxford: Oxford University Press,
       1988.
       A case study of the fate of the PCI's Historic Compromise strategy in Turin. It
       draws significant lessons about the party generally.

2.51   Ignazi, Piero. *Dal PCI al PDS.* Bologna: Mulino, 1992.
       An analysis of the transformation of the PCI into the PDS (Democratic Party of
       the Left).

2.52   Ilardi, Massimo. Accornero, Aris. Editors. *Il Partito comunista italiano: struttura
       e storica dell'organizzazione 1921/1979.* Milano: Feltrinelli, 1982.
       A good collection on the history and changing structure of the PCI.

2.53   Joll, James. *Antonio Gramsci.* Harmondsworth: Penguin, 1978.
       Gramsci for beginners.

2.54   Martinelli, Renzo. Righi, Maria Luisa. Editors. *La politica del Partito comunista
       italiano nel periodo costituente. I verbali della direzione tra il V e il VI Congresso
       1946-1948.* Roma: Fondazione Istituto Gramsci, Editori Riuniti, 1992.
       The first volume to be produced from the PCI's recently opened archive, it
       documents the decisions of the party leadership (*direzione*) during the drafting of
       the Constitution in the Constituent Assembly, 1946-1948. Essential reference point
       for all historians of the party.

2.55   Mieli, Renato. *Il PCI allo specchio. Venticinque anni di storia del comunismo italiano*. Milano: Rizzoli, 1983.
Research promoted by CERES (*Centro di studi socioeconomici*), a comprehensive historical and political analysis of the PCI. Each chapter treats a specific theme and is accompanied by a research report and useful bibliography.

2.56   Sassoon, Donald. *The Strategy of the Italian Communist Party. From the Resistance to the Historic Compromise*. London: Pinter, 1981.
A clear, if apologetic, account of the PCI's postwar strategy.

2.57   Spriano, Paolo. *Storia del Partito comunista italiano*. Torino: Einaudi, 5 volumes: Vol.1: *Da Bordiga a Gramsci* (1967); Vol.2: *Gli anni della clandestinità* (1969); Vol.3: *I fronti popolari, Stalin, la guerra* (1970); Vol.4: *La fine del fascismo. Dalla riscossa operaia alla lotta armata* (1973); Vol.5: *La Resistenza, Togliatti e il partito nuovo* (1975).
Written by the party's leading historian this is the most complete history of the party, albeit from the angle of an insider.

2.58   Urban, Joan Barth. *Moscow and the Italian Communist Party: From Togliatti to Berlinguer*. New York: Cornell Press, 1986.
A good analysis of the changing relationship between the Soviet and Italian communist parties.

Christian Democracy (DC)

2.59   Baget-Bozzo, Gianni. *Il Partito cristiano al potere. La Dc di De Gasperi e di Dosetti 1945-1954*. Firenze: Valecchi, 1974.
Essential reading on the DC in the immediate postwar period. Shows the skills of De Gasperi in positioning the DC to fill a power vacuum at the end of the war, and in laying the foundations for electoral victory.

2.60   Baget-Bozzo, Gianni. *Il Partito cristiano e l'apertura a sinistra. La Dc di Fanfani e di Moro 1954-1962*. Firenze: Valecchi, 1977.
Charts in great detail the origins of the centre-left experiment from the DC's perspective.

2.61   Cassano, Franco. *Il teorema democristiano. La mediazione della Dc nella società e nel sistema politico italiano*. Bari: De Donato, 1979.
An approach to the DC which rejects the view that it represents interests. Views the party purely as a product of its permanence in government, this in itself something largely beyond the party's control.

2.62   Einaudi, Mario. Goguel, Francois. *Christian Democracy in Italy and France*. New York: Archon, 1969.
Originally published in 1952, this is one of the earliest postwar accounts of the DC, overly sympathetic to its cause.

2.63   Follini, Marco. *L'arcipelago democristiano*. Bari: Laterza, 1990.
A good, if journalistic, analysis of Christian Democratic dominance, described here as an 'archipelago'.

2.64   Follini, Marco. *La Dc al bivio.* Bari: Laterza, 1992.
One of the last accounts of the DC before its transformation into the Italian Popular Party (PPI).

2.65   Galli, Giorgio. *Mezzo secolo di DC 1943-1993. Da De Gasperi a Mario Segni.* Milano: Rizzoli, 1993.
Standard historical work in Italian on the DC which brings together material from the author's earlier works.

2.66   Leonardi, Robert. Wertman, Douglas A. *Italian Christian Democracy: The Politics of Dominance.* New York: St. Martin's Press, 1989.
The best overview of the DC for beginners in English.

2.67   Levi, Arrigo. *La Dc nell'Italia che cambia.* Bari: Laterza, 1984.
A general work on the DC of high quality.

2.68   Malgeri, Franceso. Editor. *Storia della Democrazia cristiana.* Roma: Cinque Lune, 1978-1989, 5 vols.
The official history of the DC.

2.69   Parisi, Arturo. Editor. *Democristiani.* Bologna: Mulino, 1979.
Arguably, the best overall analysis of the DC, although it is now a little dated.

2.70   Provasi, Giancarlo. *Borghesia industriale e Democrazia Cristiana. Sviluppo economico e mediazione politica dalla ricostruzione agli anni '70.* Bari: De Donato, 1976.
Analyses the relationship between the DC and business.

2.71   Zuckerman, Alan S. *The Politics of Faction: Christian Democratic Rule in Italy.* New Haven: Yale University Press, 1979.
An excellent study of the internal politics of the DC which is fundamental to explaining the party's broader role in Italian politics.

Italian Socialism (PSI, PSDI, PSIUP)

2.72   Barnes, Samuel H. *Party Democracy: Politics in an Italian Socialist Federation.* New Haven: Yale University Press, 1967.
An early study of local faction politics in the PSI. The book still stands out for its empirical approach.

2.73   Ciofi, Paolo. Ottaviano, Franco. *Un partito per il leader. Il nuovo corso del Psi dal Midas agli anni novanta.* Messina: Rubbettino, 1990.
Good history of the PSI under former leader Bettino Craxi.

2.74   Ciuffoletti, Zeffiro. Degli'Innocenti, Maurizio. Sabbatucci, Giovanni. *Storia del Psi. III. Dal Dopoguerra a oggi.* Bari: Laterza, 1993.
The most recent history of the PSI in the postwar period, it is the third in a three volume history.

2.75   De Grand, Alexander, *The Italian Left in the Twentieth Century: A History of the Socialist and Communist Parties*. Bloomington, Indiana: Indiana University Press, 1989.
A straightforward history of the two main parties of the left.

2.76   Di Scala, Spencer M. *Renewing Italian Socialism*. Oxford: Oxford University Press, 1988.
A lengthy history which ultimately fails to inspire, but is nonetheless useful for those studying the PSI.

2.77   Galli, Giorgio. *Storia del socialismo italiano*. Bari: Laterza, 1980.
A good history of the PSI and the various groupings which split from it to form other parties.

2.78   Landolfi, Antonio. *Storia del Psi. Cent'anni di socialismo in Italia da Filippo Turati a Bettino Craxi*. Milano: SugarCo, 1990.
Good history of the PSI since its founding.

2.79   Merkel, Wolfgang. *Prima e dopo Craxi. Le trasformazioni del PSI*. Padova: Liviana Editrice, 1987.
A sophisticated analysis of the nature of the PSI and the changes it underwent under the leadership of Bettino Craxi. The best book on the PSI, it should be translated.

2.80   Miniati, Silvano. *PSIUP, 1943-72. Vita e morte di un partito*. Roma: Edimez, 1981.
History of the PSIUP, a party formed out of a split from the PSI over the centre-left experiment in the early 1960s, and adopting the name of the original socialist party.

2.81   Padellaro, Antonio. *Processo a Craxi: ascesa e declino di un leader*. Milano: Sperling & Kupfer, 1993.
Journalistic account of the rise and fall of the former leader of the PSI, Craxi.

2.82   Sabbatucci, Giovanni. General Editor. *Storia del socialismo italiano*. Roma: Il Poligono, 1980-81, 6 vols.
The most complete history of the PSI until the late 1970s. The last two volumes cover the postwar period.

2.83   Taddei, Francesca. *Il socialismo italiano del dopoguerra: correnti ideologiche e scelte politiche (1943-1947)*. Milano: Angeli, 1984.
An important study of the socialists and their divisions in the immediate postwar period when the split occurred which created the Italian Social Democratic Party (PSDI).

2.84   Tempestini, Attilio. *Il terzaforzista recidivio. Le linee e i risultati elettorali dei socialdemocratici e dei socialisti da Palazzo Barberini alle elezioni del 1968*. Torino: Stampatori, 1975.
One of the few studies of the Italian Social Democratic Party (PSDI). Includes analysis of the Italian Socialist Party, from which the PSDI was launched after a split in 1947.

The Other Parties

2.85   Allievi, Stefano. *Le parole della Lega*. Milano: Garzanti, 1992.
Account of the rise of the Northern League and its success in the 1992 national elections.

2.86   Bobbio, Luigi. *Storia di Lotta Continua*. Milano: Feltrinelli, 1988.
Adaptation of an earlier work, it is a good history of 'Continuous Struggle', one of the organisations of the extreme left in the 1960s and 1970s.

2.87   Bolla, Maria Carla. Trentini, Giancarlo. *Il Pri. L'imagine psicosociale di un partito politico*. Milano: Franco Angeli, 1983.
Interesting analysis of the make-up of the Italian Republican Party (PRI).

2.88   Borcio, R. and Lodi, G. Editors. *La sfida verde: il movimento ecologista in Italia*. Padova: Liviana Editrice, 1988.
Study of the ecologist movement in Italy.

2.89   Ciani, Arnaldo. *Il Partito liberale italiano da Croce a Malagodi*. Napoli: Edizioni Scientifiche Italiane, 1968.
History of the Italian Liberal Party (PLI) until the late 1960s.

2.90   Corbetta, Piergiorgio. Parisi, Arturo M. L. *Il voto repubblicano: alle origini del 26 giugno*. Bologna: Istituto Cattaneo, 1984.
A good sociological analysis of the Republican Party.

2.91   De Luna, Giovanni. *Storia del Partito d'Azione: la rivoluzione democratica: 1942-1947*. Milano: Feltrinelli, 1982.
The most comprehensive study of the brief life of the Action Party.

2.92   Del Carria, R. *Il potere diffuso: i verdi in Italia*. Verona: Edizioni del Movimento Nonviolento, 1986.
Study of the Italian Greens.

2.93   Diani, Mario. *Isole nell'arcipelago. Il movimento ecologista in Italia*. Bologna: Mulino, 1988.
A good study of the ecologist movement.

2.94   Diamanti, Ilvo. *La Lega: geografia, storia e sociologia di un nuovo soggetto politico*. Roma: Donzelli, 1993.
The best analysis to date of the Northern League.

2.95   Ferraresi, Franco. *The Radical Right in Italy*. Oxford: Blackwell, 1988.
A general study of the Italian far right.

2.96   Gilioli, Alessandro. *Forza Italia. La storia, gli uomini, i misteri*. Bergamo: Ferruccio Arnoldi Editore, 1994.
There are at present only journalistic accounts available of Silvio Berlusconi's party, *Forza Italia*. This is one of the better of them by a journalist from the weekly *L'Europeo*.

2.97   Ignazi, Piero. *Il polo escluso. Profilo del Movimento sociale italiano-DN (1946-1987)* Bologna: Mulino, 1989.
        The first serious study of the Italian Social Movement (MSI, neo-Fascist party).

2.98   Ignazi, Piero. *Postfascisti? Dal Movimento sociale italiano ad Alleanza nazionale.* Bologna: Mulino, 1995.
        Succinct account of the Italian Social Movement's transition to 'post-Fascist' status as the National Alliance (AN) in the early 1990s.

2.99   Mannheimer, Renato. *La Lega Lombarda* Milan: Feltrinelli, 1991.
        A good study of the rise of the Lombard League.

2.100   Marelli, Sante. *Storia dei liberali. Da Cavour a Zanone.* Rimini: Panozzo, 1985.
        The most up to date history of the Italian Liberal Party (PLI) available.

2.101   Mercuri, Lamberto. Editor. *L'Azionismo nella storia d'Italia 1946-1953.* Bologna: Società Editrice Il Lavoro Editoriale, 1988.
        Document-based history of the Action Party with introduction by Lamberto Mercuri.

2.102   Pallotta, Gino. *Il qualunquismo e l'avventura di Guglielmo Giannini.* Milano: Bompiani, 1972.
        Study of the rise and fall of the right-wing 'Everyman's' Party.

2.103   Parisi, Arturo. Varni, A. *Organizzazione e politica nel PRI: 1946-1984.* Bologna: Istituto Cattaneo, 1985.
        History of the internal politics of the Republican Party.

2.104   Parisi, Arturo M. L. Editor. *La dirigenza repubblicana.* Bologna: Istituto Cattaneo, 1987.
        An analysis of the leadership of the Republican Party.

2.105   Rossi, Gianni S. *Alternative e doppiopetto. Il Msi dalla contestazione alla Destra nazionale (1968-1973).* Roma: Istituto di Studi Corporative, 1992.
        Analysis of the revival of the far right (MSI-DN) in the early 1970s.

2.106   Setta, Sandro. *L'Uomo qualunque, 1944-1948.* Bari: Laterza, 1995.
        The most comprehensive account available of the short life of the 'Everyman's' Party.

2.107   Teodori, Massimo. Ignazi, Piero. Panebianco, Angelo. *I nuovi radicali: storia e sociologia di un movimento politico.* Milano: Mondadori, 1977.
        A good analysis of the Radical Party (PR) at the height of its notoriety.

2.108   Veciello, Walter. Editor. *I radicali. Compagni, qualunquisti, destabilizzatori?* Roma: Edizioni Quaderni Radicali, 1981.
        Interesting contributions on the nature and significance of the Radical Party (PR) in the 1970s.

2.109   Vimercati, Daniele. *I lombardi alla nuova crociata.* Milano: Marsia, 1990.
        Account of the rise of the Northern League in the 1980s.

ELECTIONS, VOTING BEHAVIOUR AND REFERENDA

2.110   AA.VV. (Various Authors). *Il comportamento elettorale in Lombardia 1946-1980.*
Firenze: Le Monnier, 1983.
An unusually detailed study of voting behaviour in the region of Lombardy in the
postwar period. Provides essential background to the rise of the Lombard League
in the 1980s.

2.111   Almond, Gabriel. Verba, Sidney. *The Civic Culture: Political Attitudes in Five
Nations.* Princeton: Princeton University Press, 1963.
Path breaking work which gave postwar Italian political culture its essential
characteristics. Modified by [2:112].

2.112   Almond, Gabriel. Verba, Sidney. *The Civic Culture Revisited.* Boston: Little
Brown, 1984.
Revisiting the theme of [2:111]. The chapter on Italy shows how the previous
characterisation needs modifying.

2.113   Barbagli, Marzio. Corbetta, Piergiorgio. Parisi, Arturo. Schadee, Hans M. A.
Fluidità elettorale e classi sociali in Italia. Bologna: Mulino, 1979.
A key text which emphasised the distinction between individual voting behaviour
and aggregate outcome, something which is fundamental to understanding changes
in Italian voting behaviour.

2.114   Barnes, Samuel H. *Representation in Italy: Institutionalized Tradition and
Electoral Choice.* Chicago: University of Chicago Press, 1977.
An exemplary work and the best portrayal in English of the subcultural model
of voting behaviour.

2.115   Bartolini, Stefano. D'Alimonte, Roberto. Editors. *Maggioritario ma non troppo.*
Bologna: Mulino, 1995.
Originally a special issue of the *Rivista Italiana di Scienza Politica* (the Italian
Political Science Association house journal), it offers a detailed analysis of the
1994 national elections and evaluates their significance.

2.116   Caciagli, Mario. Corbetta, Piergiorgio. Editors. *Elezioni regionali e sistema
politico nazionale. Italia, Spagna e Repubblica Tedesca.* Bologna: Mulino, 1987.
Part I of this book contains important chapters on regional voting behaviour in
Italy by Arturo Parisi, Raffaele De Mucci and Oreste Massoni.

2.117   Caciagli, Mario. Spreafico, Alberto. Editors. *Vent'anni di elezioni in Italia. 1968-
1987.* Padua: Liviana Editrice, 1990.
The best introduction to Italian voting behaviour from the perspective of
individual parties. Different specialists analyse the changing electoral support for
each party over a twenty year period.

2.118   Calvi, Gabriele. Vannucci, Andrea. *L'Elettore sconosciuto. Analisi socioculturale
e segmentazione degli orientamenti politici nel 1994.* Bologna: Mulino, 1995.
Using data on the social and cultural make-up of the Italians, the book argues that
the 1994 elections were characterised by considerable stability in terms of voter
choice.

2.119 Capecchi, Vittorio. Cioni Polacchini, V. Galli, Giorgio. Sivini, Giordano. *Il comportamento elettorale in Italia*. Bologna: Mulino, 1968.
An early study funded by the Carlo Cattaneo Institute which identified the stabilities of Italian voting behaviour with Italy's sub-cultures.

2.120 Cartocci, Roberto. *Elettori in Italia* Bologna: Mulino, 1990.
One of the best general introductions to Italian voting behaviour.

2.121 Chimenti, Anna. *Storia dei Referendum. Dal divorzio alla riforma elettorale*. Roma: Laterza, 1993.
One of the few histories of the use of the referendum available. Published too early to include the referenda held in 1993 and 1995.

2.122 Corbetta, Piergiorgio. Parisi, Arturo. Schadee, Hans M. A. *Elezioni in Italia. Struttura e tipologia delle consultazioni politiche*. Bologna: Mulino, 1988.
An assessment of levels of electoral volatility in the 1970s and 1980s compared with the previous two decades.

2.123 Diamanti, Ilvo. Parisi, Arturo. *Elezioni a Trieste. Identità territoriale e comportamento di voto*. Torino: Utet, 1991.
One of the few detailed local voting studies available, it explains the high levels of electoral volatility in Trieste.

2.124 Diamanti, Ilvo. Mannheimer, Renato. Editors. *Milano a Roma. Guida all'Italia elettorale del 1994*. Roma: Donzelli, 1994.
Comprehensive guide to the 1994 elections divided into four sections: the new electoral rules, parties and alliances, territorial analyses, and political communication and economic actors in the electoral market.

2.125 Mannheimer, Renato. Sani, Giacomo. *Il mercato elettorale. Identikit dell'elettore italiano*. Bologna: Mulino, 1987.
A study of the political behaviour and attitudes of the Italian electorate in the mid-1980s.

2.126 Mannheimer, Renato. *Capire il voto. Contributi per l'analisi del comportamento elettorale delle consultazioni politiche*. Milano: Franco Angeli, 1989.
One of the best introductions to Italian voting behaviour.

2.127 Mannheimer, Renato. Sani, Giacomo. *La rivoluzione elettorale. L'Italia tra la prima e la seconda repubblica* Milano: Anabasi, 1994.
Detailed analysis of the path breaking national elections of 1992 and the local elections of 1993, assessing the extent to which an 'electoral revolution' took place. Includes contributions from Paolo Natale and Mario Rodriguez.

2.128 McCarthy, Patrick. Pasquino, Gianfranco. Editors. *The End of Post-War Politics in Italy. The Landmark 1992 Elections*. Boulder: Westview Press, 1993.
The first book-length analysis of Italian national elections in English since the American Enterprise Institute volume on the 1979 elections [2.135]. This alone is indicative of the significance of these elections in reflecting the profound changes at work in Italian politics in the early 1990s.

2.129 Messina, Sebastiano. *La grande riforma*. Bari: Laterza, 1993.
The best summary of the debate on electoral reform. Published too early,
however, to take account of the new electoral system introduced in 1993.

2.130 Noiret, Serge. Editor. *Political strategies and Electoral Reforms: Origins of
Voting Systems in Europe in the 19th. and 20th. Centuries*. Baden-Baden: Nomos
Verlagsgesellschaft, 1990.
The substantial chapter by Harmut Ullrich is the most comprehensive history of
the Italian electoral system available.

2.131 Novelli, S. *Il voto amministrativo democristiano*. Bologna: Mulino, 1981.
Detailed analysis of the DC's local vote.

2.132 Parisi, Arturo M. L. Pasquino, Gianfranco. *Continuità e movimento elettorale in
Italia*. Bologna: Mulino, 1977.
A pioneering introduction to Italian voting behaviour, it established the classic
three-fold schema of *voto d'opinione*, *voto di scambio* and *voto di appartenenza*.

2.133 Parisi, Arturo M. L. *Mobilità senza movimento*. Bologna: Mulino, 1980.
Important contribution to the 1980s debate on stabilities in Italian voting
behaviour.

2.134 Pasquino, Gianfranco. *Votare un solo candidato. Le conseguenze politiche della
preferenza unica*. Bologna: Mulino, 1993.
Analysis of the political consequences of the modification of preference voting
(achieved in the referendum of 1991).

2.135 Penniman, Howard R. (1987, 1981, 1977) Editor. *Italy at the Polls, 1976, 1979,
1983*. Washington: American Enterprise Institute, 1977, 1981, 1987 (3 separate
volumes).
The best analyses in English of national elections in Italy up to and including the
1983 elections. No volumes appeared thereafter suggesting that the series has been
discontinued. A volume in English on the 1992 elections was published by
Westview [2.128], and one in Italian on the 1994 elections was published by
Mulino [2.115].

2.136 Scaramozzino, Pasquale. *Un'analisi statistica del voto di preferenza in Italia*.
Milano: Giuffré, 1979.
Statistical analysis of the effects of preference voting.

2.137 Spreafico, Alberto. LaPalombara, Joseph. *Elezioni e comportamento politico*.
Milano: Comunità, 1963.
The best of the early psephological studies before the Cattaneo-funded studies of
the late 1960s.

2.138 Statera, Gianni. *Come votano gli italiani. Dal bipartitismo imperfetto alla crisi del
sistema politico*. Milano: Sperling & Kupfer, 1993.
An analysis of electoral change in the 1980s and early 1990s, culminating in the
1992 national elections.

2.139 Warner, Steven. Gambetta, Diego. *La retorica della riforma. Fine del sistema proporzionale in Italia*. Torino: Einaudi, 1994.
Argues that it is almost impossible to change the electoral system and achieve specific desired political outcomes from it. Places the debate over electoral reform in the early 1990s in a broader perspective, and includes an excellent introduction on the theory of electoral systems.

CLIENTELISM AND CORRUPTION

2.140 Allum, Percy A. *Politics and Society in Post-War Naples* Cambridge: Cambridge University Press, 1973.
Essential reading to understand the DC's power structure in the south of Italy.

2.141 Barbacetto, G. Veltri, E. *Milano degli scandali*. Bari: Laterza, 1991.
An account of the corruption exposure in Milan uncovered before the 1992 elections.

2.142 Barca, Luciano. Trento, S. Editors. *L'Economia della corruzione*. Bari: Laterza, 1994.
Good collection exploring the mechanics of political corruption.

2.143 Caciagli, Mario. Et al. *Democrazia cristiana e potere nel Mezzogiorno: il sistema democristiano a Catania*. Firenze: Guaraldi, 1977.
Case study of the DC's power base in Catania.

2.144 Caferna, Vito Marino. *Il sistema della corruzione. Le ragioni. I soggetti. I luoghi*. Bari: Laterza, 1992.
A general analysis of the system of political corruption operated by the Italian parties.

2.145 Carlucci, A. *Tangentomani. Storie, affari e tutti i documenti sui barbari che hanno saccheggiato Milano*. Milano: Baldini & Castoldi, 1992.
Good source of information on the corruption exposure in Milan in the early 1990s. It will obviously date as the trials continue.

2.146 Cazzola, Franco. Editor. *Anatomià del potere DC: enti pubblici e 'centralità democristiana'*. Bari: De Donato, 1979.
An illuminating study of the DC's penetration of the state and creation of the so-called *parastate*.

2.147 Cazzola, Franco. *Della corruzione: fisiologia e patologia di un sistema politico*. Bologna: Mulino, 1988.
Historical overview of corruption in Italy over a hundred years.

2.148 Chubb, Judith. *Patronage, Power and Poverty in Southern Italy: A Tale of Two Cities*. Cambridge: Cambridge University Press, 1982.
A brilliant case study of machine politics in Naples and Palermo which has not been bettered since.

2.149 D'Alberti, Marco. Finocchi, Renato. Editors. *Corruzione e sistema istituzionale.* Bologna: Mulino, 1994.
Excellent volume in Mulino's series 'Organizzazione e funzionamento della pubblica amministrazione'. A broad range of contributions on the operation and exposure of corruption and the penal problems associated with it.

2.150 Della Porta, Donatella. *Lo scambio occulto: casi di corruzione politica in Italia.* Bologna: Mulino, 1992.
Three case studies of corruption in local government in the 1980s.

2.151 Della Porta, Donatella. Vannucci, Alberto. *Corruzione politica e amministrazione pubblica. Risorse, meccanismi, attori.* Bologna: Mulino, 1994.
Excellent volume in Mulino's series 'Organizzazione e funzionamento della pubblica amministrazione'. Detailed examination of the dynamics of political corruption in the Italian bureaucracy.

2.152 Graziano, Luigi. *Clientelismo e sistema politico. Il caso .dell'Italia.* Milano: Franco Angeli, 1979.
First rate study of the DC's clientelistic power base in Salerno.

2.153 Gribaudi, Gabriella. *Mediatori. Antropologia del potere nel Mezzogiorno.* Torino: Rosenberg & Sellier, 1980.
Study of the local DC elites in the South, with introductory comments by Augusto Graziani and Edoardo Grendi.

2.154 Orfei, Ruggero. *L'occupazione del potere. I democristiani 1945-1975.* Milano: Longanesi, 1976.
Analysis of the DC's 'occupation' of the state over a thirty year period.

2.155 Silj, Alessandro. *Malpaese. Criminalità, corruzione e politica nell'Italia della prima Repubblica 1943-1994.* Roma: Donzelli, 1994.
History of political corruption in postwar Italy.

2.156 Tamburrano, Giuseppe. *L'iceberg democristiano.* Milano: SugarCo, 1974.
Analysis of the DC's colonisation of the state apparatus.

2.157 Turone, Sergio. *Politica ladra. Storia della corruzione in Italia 1861-1992.* Bari: Laterza, 1992.
History of political corruption in Italy since Unification.

2.158 Turani, G. Sasso, C. *I saccheggiatori. Milano: facevano i politici ma erano dei ladri.* Milano: Sperling & Kupfer, 1992.
An interesting account of the first few months of the anti-corruption enquiries of the early 1990s.

2.159 White, Caroline. *Patrons and Partisans: A Study of Politics in Two Southern Italian Communities.* Cambridge: Cambridge University Press, 1980.
A study of political elites and clientele politics in Christian Democrat and Communist-dominated villages in the Abruzzi, it brings out some illuminating comparisons between the two parties.

3

Government

EXECUTIVE AND LEGISLATURE

3.1 Amato, Giuliano. *Una Repubblica da riformare*. Bologna: Mulino, 1980.
One of the earlier books on institutional reform by an observant academic and politician, who was Prime Minister 1992-1993.

3.2 Amato, Giuliano. Barbera, Augusto. Editors. *Manuale di diritto pubblico*. Bologna: Mulino, 1984.
Contains more than the title suggests, with chapters on a wide range of aspects of the Italian institutional system, including the President, government, bureaucracy, legal system.

3.3 Baldassare, A. Mezzanotte, C. *Gli uomini del Quirinale. Da De Nicola a Pertini* Bari: Laterza, 1985.
The only book-length study of the little understood role of the presidency.

3.4 Bonanni, Massimo (Editor). Avril, Pierre. Stacey, Frank. *Governi, ministri, presidente. Competenze dei ministri, collegialità del governo e funzioni del premier nell'esperienza di tre esecutivi europei: un contributo allo studio del governo in Italia*. Milano: Edizione di Comunità, 1978.
An interesting approach to resolving Italy's institutional problems, the book contains analyses of the functioning of the executive in France, Britain and the European Community. The editor draws out the lessons for Italy, although there is little on the Italian system itself.

3.5 Calandra, Piero. *Il Governo della Repubblica*. Bologna: Mulino, 1986.
One of the best overviews of the functioning of the government and executive.

3.6 Calise, Mauro. Mannheimer, Renato. *Governanti in Italia. Un trentennio repubblicano 1946-1976*. Bologna: Mulino, 1982.
One of the few empirical analyses of the elites in government and the executive.

3.7 Cassese, Sabino. *Esiste un governo in Italia?* Rome: Officina, 1988.
One of the best general overviews of the working of the government and executive.

3.8   Cotta, Maurizio. *Classe politica e parlamento in Italia: 1946-1976.* Bologna: Mulino, 1979.
One of the few studies of the political elites in parliament.

3.9   Di Palma, Giuseppe. *Surviving Without Governing: the Italian Parties in Parliament.* Berkeley: University of California Press, 1977.
Now famous for its portrayal of a delegitimised and malfunctioning parliament. Partially uses Sartori's framework of analysis of party systems.

3.10   Fusaro, Carlo. *Guida alle riforme istituzionali. Per capire le proposte di cui si parla.* Catanzaro: Rubettino Editore, 1992.
A guide to the institutional reform debate, particularly the various reforms proposed (and which failed) during the 1987-92 legislature.

3.11   Manzella, Andrea. *Il Parlamento.* Bologna: Mulino, 1991, 2nd. Edition.
The most up-to-date and detailed analysis of the Italian parliament, its rules and procedures, and one that gives the institution greater centrality than previously assumed.

3.12   Pasquino, Gianfranco. *Restituire lo scettro al principe. Proposte di riforme istituzionale.* Bari: Laterza, 1985.
Written by one of the key protagonists in the institutional reform debate, it not only gives a clear summary of it but is a useful critique of the functioning of the Italian political system.

3.13   Pitruzzella, Giovanni. *La presidenza del Consiglio dei ministri e l'organizzazione del governo.* Padova: Cedam, 1986.
Useful, if legalistic, account of the role of the Italian Prime Minister and cabinet.

3.14   Predieri, Alberto. Editor. *Il parlamento nel sistema politico italiano.* Milano: Comunità, 1975.
Useful collection on the functioning of parliament in the 1970s.

3.15   Ristucci, Sergio. Editor. *L'istituzione governo: analisi e prospettive.* Milano: Edizioni di Comunità, 1977.
Good analysis of the functioning of the main institutions, with a particular focus on the executive.

3.16   Ruggeri, Antonio. *Il Consiglio dei ministri nella costituzione italiana.* Milano: Giuffré, 1981.
Legalistic but informative account of the role of the Prime Minister and cabinet.

3.17   Sartori, Giovanni. Editor. *Il Parlamento italiano 1946-1963.* Napoli: Edizioni Scientifiche Italiane, 1963.
Early work on the parliament funded by the Cattaneo Institute.

3.18   Spagna Musso, Enrico. Editor. *Costituzione e strutture del governo: il problema della presidenza del Consiglio.* Padova: Cedam, 1979-82, 2 vols.
Detailed analyses of different aspects of the role of the Prime Minister. Most of the contributions are legally-oriented.

3.19   Venditti, Roberto. *Il manuale Cencelli: il prontuario della lottizzazione democristiana.* Roma: Editori Riuniti, 1981.
Detailed analysis of the dynamics of government coalition formation. Cencelli was the Christian Democrat who designed the 'rules' governing the distribution of ministries among the governing parties.

3.20   Ventura, Luigi. *Il governo a multipolarità diseguale.* Milano: Giuffré, 1988.
Good general analysis of the functioning of Italian government and policy-making.

JUDICIARY AND LEGAL SYSTEM

3.21   Canosa, Romano. Federico, Pietro. *La magistratura in Italia dal 1945 a oggi.* Bologna: Mulino, 1974.
A good overview of the role of the judiciary until the 1970s.

3.22   Cappelletti, Mauro. Merryman, J. H. Perillo, J. *The Italian Legal System.* Stanford: Stanford University Press, 1967.
Dated but still useful text on the legal system.

3.23   Certoma, G. L. *The Italian Legal System.* London: Butterworth, 1985.
The most extensive treatment of the legal system.

3.24   *Enciclopedia del diritto.* Milano: Giuffré, 1958-.
Useful guide to Italian law and the legal system.

3.25   Freddi, Giorgio. *Tensioni e conflitto nella magistratura. Un'analisi istituzionale dal dopoguerra al 1968.* Bari: Laterza, 1977.
Good analysis of the internal politics and factions of the judiciary.

3.26   Guarnieri, Carlo. *L'indipendenza della magistratura.* Padova: Cedam, 1981.
Evaluates the degree of autonomy enjoyed by the judiciary in the 1970s.

3.27   Guarnieri, Carlo. *Magistratura e politica in Italia.* Bologna: Mulino, 1993.
One of the best books to have appeared on the judiciary and its relationship with politicians and the political system.

3.28   Pappalardo, Sergio. *Gli iconoclasti. Magistratura democratica nel quadro della associazione nazionale magistrati.* Milano: Angeli, 1987.
A study of the left wing faction which emerged in the judiciary in the 1970s under the name Democratic Magistrates.

3.29   Pizzorusso, Alessandro. *L'organizzazione della giustizia in Italia. La magistratura nel sistema politico e istituzionale.* Torino: Einaudi, 1982.
The best analysis of the structure and power of the judiciary and its relationship with other institutions of the state.

3.30   Rodotà, Stefano. *La corte costituzionale.* Rome: Editori Riuniti, 1986.
The best account of the structures and power of the Constitutional Court.

3.31   Zannotti, F. *La magistratura. Un gruppo di pressione istituzionale.* Padova: Cedam, 1989.
A good study of the judiciary from a social science perspective.

SUB-NATIONAL GOVERNMENT AND CENTRE-PERIPHERY RELATIONS

3.32   *Annuario delle autonomie locali.* Roma: Edizione delle Autonomie, 1981-.
Yearbook providing essential data and other reference material on Italian sub-national governments.

3.33   Bettin, Gianfranco. Magnier, Annick. *Chi governa la città? Una ricerca sugli assessori comunali.* Padova: Cedam, 1991.
Study of the role and performance of local councillors.

3.34   Cazzola, Franco. *Periferici integrati. Chi, dove, quando nelle amministrazioni comunali.* Bologna: Mulino, 1991.
In-depth analysis of local government.

3.35   Dente, Bruno. *Governare la frammentazione. Stato, regioni, ed enti locali in Italia.* Bologna: Mulino, 1985.
The best overview in a single volume of centre-periphery relations and sub-national government.

3.36   Fried, Robert C. *The Italian Prefects: a Study in Administrative Politics.* New Haven: Yale University Press, 1963.
The best account available of the former prefectoral system, based on the Napoleonic model.

3.37   Istituto per la scienza dell'amministrazione pubblica (ISAP). *La regionalizzazione.* Milano: Giuffré, 1983, 2 vols.
The most comprehensive historical and institutional analysis of regional government, which also draws comparisons with some other countries.

3.38   Istituto per la scienza dell'amministrazione pubblica (ISAP). *Le relazioni centro-periferia.* Milano: Giuffré, 1984, 3 vols.
The most comprehensive analysis of centre-periphery relations, displaying both the traditional legalistic approach as well as more recent social scientific methods of analysis.

3.39   Leonardi, Robert. Putnam, Robert D. Nanetti, Raffaella Y. *Il Caso Basilicata: l'effetto regione dal 1970 al 1986.* Bologna: Mulino, 1987.
In-depth study of the performance of Basilicata since the introduction of its regional government.

3.40   Leonardi, Robert. Nanetti, Raffaella Y. *The Regions and European Integration. The Case of Emilia-Romagna.* London: Pinter, 1991.
Brings together specialists who analyse the political, social and economic bases which make up the so-called 'Emilian model' of development in the broader context of European political and economic integration.

3.41   Merloni, Francesco. Santatonio, Vincenzo. Torchia, Luisa. *Le funzioni del governo locale in Italia. Vol. 1. Il dato normativo.* Milano: Giuffré, 1988.
First of a two volume study of the performance of local government in Italy, this examines the basic structures and functions. See [3:42] for volume 2.

3.42   Mannozzi, S. Visco Commandini, V. *Le funzioni del governo locale in Italia. Vol. 2. Verifica dell'effettività.* Milano: Giuffré, 1990.
Second volume in an empirical study of the performance and effectiveness of local government. See [3:41] for first volume.

3.43   Maltinti, Giovanni. Petretto, Alessandro. Editors. *Finanziamento ed efficienza della spesa pubblica locale.* Torino: Giapicchelli, 1987.
Good empirical analysis of the performance of Italian local government.

3.44   Putnam, Robert D. Leonardi, Robert. Nanetti, Raffaella Y. *La pianta e le radici. Il radicamento dell'istituto regionale nel sistema politico italiano.* Bologna: Mulino, 1985.
Path breaking study of the institutionalisation of regional governments since 1970, providing valuable insights into the general question of institutional performance. This book provided the basis for Putnam's seminal work *Making Democracy Work* [2.20].

3.45   Tarrow, Sidney. *Between Center and Periphery: Grassroots Politicians in Italy and France.* New Haven: Yale University Press, 1977.
A significant work in comparative politics which highlights the nature of the links between centre and periphery in Italy by comparing them with those in France. The book brings out the importance of the role of parties in Italy.

ADMINISTRATION AND CIVIL SERVICE

3.46   AA.VV. *Il potere militare in Italia.* Bari: Laterza, 1971.
Useful collection on the army.

3.47   Bianchi, Gianfranco. *L'Italia dei ministeri: lo sfascio guidato.* Roma: Editori Riuniti, 1981.
Journalistic and highly readable account of the malfunctioning of the bureaucracy.

3.48   Canosa, Romano. *La polizia in Italia dal 1945 ad oggi.* Bologna: Mulino, 1976.
One of the few texts on the role of the police in the postwar period.

3.49   Cassese, Sabino. Editor. *L'amministrazione pubblica in Italia.* Bologna: Mulino, 1974.
Excellent collection on the Italian bureaucracy, if a little dated.

3.50   Cassese, Sabino. *Questione amministrativa e questione meridionale. Dimensioni e reclutamento della burocrazia dall'Unità ad oggi.* Milano: Giuffré, 1977.
Focuses on the recruitment policy and composition of the civil service. Evaluates the effects on performance of the bureaucracy being staffed mainly by people from the South.

3.51   Cassesse, Sabino. *Il sistema amminstrativo italiano*. Bologna: Mulino, 1983.
       The best overview of the Italian administrative system.

3.52   Cassesse, Sabino. Editor. *L'amministrazione centrale*. Torino: Utet, 1984.
       An excellent collection on the bureaucracy.

3.53   Cassesse, Sabino. *Le basi del diritto amministrativo*. Torino: Einaudi, 1989.
       A general book on administrative law, but with a primary focus on the Italian
       administrative system and its evolution. Meticulous approach to the subject.

3.54   Cercora, G. Editor. *Il pubblico impiego: struttura e retribuzioni*. Bologna:
       Mulino, 1991.
       Detailed treatment of public sector employment.

3.55   Cerquetti, Enea. *Le forze armate dal 1945 al 1975. Strutture e dottrine*.
       Milano: Feltrinelli, 1975.
       An account of the postwar development of the armed forces, emphasising the
       influence of the Cold War and the assistance of the United States.

3.56   Ceva, Lucio. *Le forze armate*. Torino: Utet, 1981.
       Volume XI of Utet's *Storia della società italiana dall'Unità a oggi* provides a
       useful history of the armed forces, but only has a short epilogue on the period of
       the Republic.

3.57   Collin, R. *The De Lorenzo Gambit: the Italian coup manqué of 1964*. Beverly
       Hills: Sage, 1977.
       Journalistic examination of the *coup* plot of 1964.

3.58   D'Alberti, Marco. Editor. *La dirigenza pubblica*. Bologna: Mulino, 1990.
       Detailed treatment of public sector employment at national and sub-national levels.

3.59   D'Orsi, Angelo. *Il potere repressivo. La polizia. Le forze dell'ordine italiano*.
       Milano: Feltrinelli, 1972.
       One of the few books on the police force, now rather dated.

3.60   De Lutiis, Giuseppe. *Storia dei servizi segreti in Italia*. Rome: Officina, 1984.
       Detailed history of the secret services which beginners will find complex and
       difficult.

3.61   Dogan, Mattei. Editor. *The Mandarins of Western Europe*. New York: Sage,
       1975.
       Contains the findings of one of the few empirical surveys of Italian civil servants
       in comparison with their British and German equivalents. Robert Putnam used the
       distinction between 'classical' and 'political' bureaucrats to compare the three
       countries and found Italian civil servants to be consistently closer to the former
       category.

3.62   Ferraresi, Franco. *Burocrazia e politica in Italia*. Bologna: Mulino, 1980.
       Examination of the close relationship between the bureaucratic and political
       spheres.

3.63   Giannini, Massimo Severo. *Istituzioni di diritto amministrativo*. Milano: Giuffré, 1982.
       One of the most comprehensive accounts of the administration available. Adopts a legalistic approach.

3.64   Gorrieri, Ermano. *La giungla retributiva*. Bologna: Mulino, 1972.
       An analysis of the myriad of rules and regulations governing pay and conditions in the civil service.

3.65   *Istituto centrale di statistica* (ISTAT). *Statistiche sulla amministrazione pubblica*. Roma: ISTAT, various years.
       Regular publication containing comprehensive statistical data on central and subnational administrations.

3.66   Mack Smith, Dennis. *Italy and its Monarchy*. New Haven: Yale University Press, 1989.
       One of the few texts in English to provide an overview of the history and role of the Italian monarchy.

3.67   Pennella, G. Editor. *La produttività nella pubblica amministrazione: rapporto al Consiglio nazionale dell'economia e del lavoro*. Milano: Edizioni del Sole-24 ore, 1987.
       Volume 3 in a study of productivity in Italy, this focuses on Italian ministries and other agencies of government. The findings (very poor levels of productivity) fit the conventional wisdom.

3.68   Ruffilli, Roberto. (Edited by Maria Serena Piretti). *Istituzioni, società, stato*. Bologna: Mulino, 1989-1991. Vol. 1: *Il ruolo delle istituzioni amministrative nella formazione dello stato in Italia*. Vol. 2: *Nascita e crisi dello stato moderno: ideologie e istituzioni*. Vol. 3: *Le trasformazioni della democrazia: dalla Costituente alla progettazione delle riforme istituzionali*.
       The writings of one of the leading historians of Italian bureaucracy. Vol. 3 is on the postwar period.

3.69   Rusciani, M. *L'impiego pubblico in italia*. Bologna: Mulino, 1978.
       Interesting survey of Italian public sector employment.

3.70   Spagna Musso, Enrico. Editor. *Costituzione e struttura del governo: la riforma dei ministeri*. Padova: Cedam, 1984, 2 vols.
       Good analysis of ministerial structures of government.

3.71   Travaglio, Sergio. Editor. *Come funziona l'Italia*. Milano: Sperling and Kupfer, 1994.
       A basic alphabetic guide to all the institutions of state, accompanied by tables and statistics.

3.72   Whittam, J. *The Politics of the Italian Army*. London: Croom Helm, 1977.
       One of the few accounts in English of the Italian army and the role of politics in its functioning.

PUBLIC AND SEMI-PUBLIC BODIES

3.73   Gerelli, E. Boghetti, G. Editors. *La crisi delle partecipazioni statali: motivi e prospettivi.* Milano: Franco Angeli, 1981.
Good analysis of the state-holding companies and their crisis in the 1970s.

3.74   Holland, Stuart. *The State as Entrepreneur: New Dimensions for Public Enterprise: the IRI State Share-Holding Formula.* London: Wiedenfeld & Nicholson, 1972.
Although dated, this is the best encapsulation in English of the so-called 'IRI model' of public enterprise.

3.75   Maggia, G. Fornengo, G. *Appunti sul sistema delle partecipazioni statali.* Torino: Einaudi, 1976.
Analysis of the 'state participation' system and its network of special agencies.

3.76   Mortara, Alberto. (Introduced by). *Gli enti pubblici italiani. Anagrafe legislazione e giurisprudenza dal 1861 al 1970.* Milano: Ciriec/Franco Angeli, 1972.
The most complete survey undertaken of Italian public agencies, published as part of the 'Ciriec Collana' series, no. 9.

3.77   Posner, M. V. Woolf, Stuart J. *Italian Public Enterprise.* London: Duckworth, 1967.
Although dated, this is a good general overview in English of the system of public enterprises.

3.78   Saraceno, P. *Il sistema delle impresa partecipazione statale.* Milano: Giuffré, 1975.
Informative account of the so-called 'state participation' system of semi-public companies.

3.79   Serrani, Donatello. *Il potere per enti: enti pubblici e sistema politico in Italia.* Bologna: Mulino, 1978.
Comprehensive analysis of the system of public enterprises and how they relate to the political system.

PUBLIC POLICIES AND DOMESTIC POLICY-MAKING

3.80   Amato, Giuliano. *Il governo dell'industria in Italia.* Bologna: Mulino, 1971.
Regarded as seminal in its examination of the relationship between the economy and the political system. The book generated extensive research by others.

3.81   Amato, Giuliano. *Economia, politica, istituzioni.* Bologna: Mulino, 1976.
One of the first significant general interpretations of Italian policy-making, based on the idea of a 'spoils-distributing' government.

3.82   Amendola, Giorgio. Botré, C. *Italia inquinata.* Roma: Editori Riuniti, 1978.
An account of the ecological destruction which has occurred in Italy.

98   Bibliography

3.83   Amendola, Giorgio. Canata, P. G. Conti, L. Degli, P. Espinasa, F. Giovenale,
       Karrer, F., Libertini, M. Nebbia, G. Pinchera, G. Reallici, E. *Il malpaese:
       rapporto sull'ambiente.* Roma: Ediesse and Lega per L'ambiente, 1983.
       The most comprehensive account of the environment and pollution.

3.84   Ardigò, Achille. Barbano, F. Editors. *Medici e sociosanitari: professioni in
       transizione.* Milano: Franco Angeli, 1981.
       Documents the changes in the National Health Service contained in the reforms
       of 1978 and their effects.

3.85   Ardigò, Achille. Editor. *Per una rifondazione del welfare state.* Milano: Franco
       Angeli, 1985.
       Analysis of the welfare state and proposed solutions to its problems.

3.86   Ascoli, Ugo. Editor. *Welfare state all'italiana.* Bari: Laterza, 1984.
       Collection on the welfare state with an emphasis on its clientelistic and patronage-
       based nature.

3.87   Castellino, Onorato. *Il labrinto delle pensioni.* Bologna: Mulino, 1976.
       Analysis of the pensions system, including a full listing of the numerous agencies
       and institutions making up the system.

3.88   Cazzola, Giuliano. *Lo stato sociale tra crisi e riforme: il caso Italia.* Bologna:
       Mulino, 1994.
       Analysis of the welfare state, including reference to important changes which
       occurred after 1992.

3.89   Cherubini, Arnaldo. *Storia della previdenza sociale in Italia (1860-1960).* Roma:
       Editori Riuniti, 1977.
       History of the social security system.

3.90   Dente, Bruno. *Le politiche pubbliche in Italia,* Bologna: Mulino, 1990.
       The best general overview of public policy-making.

3.91   Dente, Bruno. *Politiche pubbliche e pubblica amministrazione.* Rimini: Maggioli,
       1990.
       Good collection on public policy-making and implementation.

3.92   Fadiga Zanatta, Anna Laura. *Il sistema scolastico italiano.* Bologna: Mulino,
       1971.
       Excellent account of the school system, if now a little dated.

3.93   Fausto, Domenicantonio. *Il sistema italiano di sicurezza sociale.* Bologna:
       Mulino, 1978.
       History and analysis of the organisational and financial structure of the social
       security system.

3.94   Ferrera, Maurizio. *Il welfare state in Italia: sviluppo e crisi in prospettiva
       comparata.* Bologna: Mulino, 1984.
       Arguably the best book to have appeared on the welfare state. An English
       synthesis of the work has also been published [3.97].

3.95   Ferrera, Maurizio. *Modelli di solidarità: politica e riforme sociali nelle democrazie*. Bologna: Mulino, 1993.
A major comparative text which seeks to explain the differences in scope of welfare states (i.e. which people are covered by benefits). Contains a specific section on the Italian case.

3.96   Ferrera, Maurizio. Zincone, Giovanna. Editors. *Le salute che noi pensiamo: domande sanitaria e politiche pubbliche in Italia*. Bologna: Mulino, 1986.
Analyses the organisational impact of the changes in the National Health Service since 1978.

3.97   Flora, Peter. Editor. *Growth to Limits. The Western European Welfare States Since World War II*. Berlin: De Gruyter, 1987.
Vol 2, pp.388-499, of this multi-volumed series contains a substantial contribution on Italy by Maurizio Ferrera which is a synthesis and translation of the author's Italian book on the subject [3.94].

3.98   Freddi, Giorgio. Editor. *Rapporto Perkoff*. Bologna: Mulino, 1984.
Good collection on the changes in the National Health Service ushered in by the 1978 reforms and their effects.

3.99   Fubini, A. *Urbanistica in Italia*. Bologna: Mulino, 1976.
Analysis of town planning in the postwar period.

3.100   Furlong, Paul. *Modern Italy. Representation and Reform*. London: Routledge, 1994.
An introduction to Italian public policy-making which outlines the historical development of the state and then adopts a comparative framework within which to view the Italian case.

3.101   Greco, N. *La valutazione di impatto ambientale: rivoluzione o compilazione amministrativa?* Milano: Franco Angeli, 1984.
Analyses the administrative and political dynamics at work behind environmental policy.

3.102   ISTAT. *Statistiche ambientali*. Roma: Istituto Nazionale di Statistica, 1984, 2 vols.
Comprehensive data on the environment gathered by the National Institute of Statistics.

3.103   Leone, U. *Geografia per l'ambiente*. Roma: La Nuova Italia Scientifica, 1987.
Account of the environment and pollution.

3.104   Lewansky, R. *Il controllo degli inquinamenti delle acque: l'attuazione di una politica pubblica*. Milano: Giuffré, 1986.
Excellent policy-making case study focusing on water pollution.

3.105   Livolsi, L. Et al. *La macchina del vuoto*. Bologna: Mulino, 1974.
General evaluation of educational policy.

3.106 Rochat, G. Sateriale, G. Spano, L. *La casa in Italia, 1945-80. Alle radici del potere democristiano.* Bologna: Zanichelli, 1980.
Fascinating account of housing policy and its partisan use. Includes useful statistical appendix.

3.107 Morisi, M. *Parlamento e politiche pubbliche.* Roma: Lavoro, 1988.
Good analysis of parliament's role in the public policy-making process.

3.108 Padoa Schioppa, Fiorella. *Scuola e classi sociali.* Bologna: Mulino, 1974.
Analysis of educational policies.

FOREIGN POLICY AND EUROPEAN INTEGRATION

3.109 Aliboni, Roberto. Editor. *Southern European Security in the 1990s.* London: Pinter, 1992.
In the absence of any single volume on Italian security policy, the chapter by Greco and Guazzone in this volume is a useful resource.

3.110 Bonanni, Massimo. *La politica estera della repubblica italiana.* Milano: Comunità, 1967.
Early work on Italian foreign policy.

3.111 Bosworth, Richard J. B. Romano, Sergio. *La Politica Estera Italiana: 1860-1985.* Bologna: Mulino, 1991.
Charts the continuities in foreign policy from Unification to the 1980s.

3.112 Chipman, John. Editor. *NATO's Southern Allies: Internal and External Challenges.* London: Routledge, 1988.
In the absence of a single volume on Italian security policy, the chapter by Cremasco in this volume provides a good analysis.

3.113 Di Nolfo, Ennio. *Editor. Power in Europe? II. Great Britain, France, Germany and Italy and the Origins of the EEC, 1952-1957.* Berlin: De Gruyter, 1992.
Volume II of a new series of texts on European integration, this volume contains extensive information on Italy based on archive material.

3.114 Francioni, Francesco. Editor. *Italy and EC Membership Evaluated.* London: Pinter, 1992.
A dozen specialists analyse the various paradigms of the European Community in relation to Italy.

3.115 Galante, Saverio. *Il Partito comunista italiano e l'integrazione europea.* Padova: Liviana Editrice, 1988.
Analysis of the Italian Communist Party's changing views on European integration.

3.116 Graziano, Luigi. *La politica estera italiana nel dopoguerra.* Padova: Marsilio, 1968.
An early text on Italian foreign policy covering the period 1946-1967.

3.117 Istituto Affari Internazionali. *L'Italia nella politica internazionale*. Milano: Edizioni di Comunità, 1972-.
An informative yearbook on Italy's international relations.

3.118 *L'Italia e Europa. Rivista Trimestrale di Diritto, Economia, Politica, Società*. Roma: Istituto Italiano di Studi Legislativi, Maggioli Editore, 1980.
Useful yearbook on Italy's changing relations with the European Union and European states.

3.119 Kogan, Norman. *The Politics of Italian Foreign Policy*. New York: Praeger, 1963.
Early work which outlines the various actors and influences at work in the shaping of Italian foreign policy.

3.120 Lipgens, Walter. Roth, Wilfred. Editors. *Documents on the History of European Integration. Vol. 3: The Struggle for European Union by Political Parties and Interest Groups in Western European Countries 1945-1950*. Berlin: De Gruyter, 1988.
Contains an important and extensive study by Sergio Pistone of Italian pressure groups and political parties in the discussion on European integration.

3.121 Petrilli, Giuseppe. *La politica estera ed europea di De Gasperi*. Roma: Cinque Lune, 1976.
A study of De Gasperi's foreign policy with an emphasis on his European commitment.

3.122 Pistone, Sergio. Editor. *L'Italia e l'unità europea. Dalle premesse storiche all'elezione del Parlamento europeo*. Torino: Loescher, 1982.
Useful collection of key historical documents on Italy's approach to European integration.

3.123 Ronzitti, Natalino. Editor. *La politica estera italiana. Autonomia, interdipendenza, integrazione e sicurezza*. Varese: Istituto Affari Internazionali e Edizioni di Comunità, 1977.
One of the most comprehensive accounts of Italian foreign policy although the changes of the 1980s make the text rather dated.

3.124 Santoro, Carlo M. *La politica estera di una media potenza. L'Italia dall'Unità ad oggi*. Bologna: Mulino, 1991.
The best book for an up to date account of Italian foreign policy. Good historical overview followed by an analysis of the key actors making up the 'foreign policy community'.

3.125 Vannicelli, Primo. *Italy, NATO and the European Community*. Cambridge: Cambridge University Press, 1974.
Interesting analysis of Italy's foreign relations, but dated.

3.126 Walker, Richard. *Dal confronto al consenso. I partiti politici italiani e l'integrazione europeo*. Roma: Istituto Affari Internazionali, 1976.
An overview of the changing positions of the Italian parties on the question of European integration up until the mid-1970s.

3.127 Willis, Roy F. *Italy Chooses Europe*. Oxford: Oxford University Press, 1971. A detailed, but largely descriptive, account of Italy's approach to the idea of European unity in the immediate postwar period and its eventual accession to the European Community.

4

Economy

GENERAL WORKS

4.1 Allen, Kevin J. Stevenson, A. A. *An Introduction to the Italian Economy.* London: Martin Robertson, 1975.
The best introduction in English to the postwar Italian economy.

4.2 *Banco d'Italia.* Roma: *Banco d'Italia*, Various Years.
The Bank of Italy's annual reports provide a useful guide to the economy.

4.3 Bianchi, Carluccio. Casarosa, Carlo. Editors. *The Recent Performance of the Italian Economy. Market Outcomes and State Policy.* Milano: Franco Angeli, 1991.
Collection of specialist analyses deriving from an international conference.

4.4 Battaglia, Adolfo. Valcamonici, Roberto. Editors. *Nella competizione globale. Una politica industriale verso il 2000.* Laterza: Bari, 1990.
The most up to date analysis of the state of the Italian economy and of its prospects in the European single market.

4.5 *Confindustria.* Roma: *Confindustria*, Various Years.
Annual reports of the general employers' federation provide a good guide to the changing economy.

4.6 *Economist.* London: Economist Publications, Various Years.
Annual survey on Italy and occasional specialist surveys.

4.7 *Economist Intelligence Unit* (EIU). London: EIU, Various Years.
Quarterly and Annual Reports and occasional special reports on Italy.

4.8 *Financial Times.* London: Financial Times Publications, Various Years.
Annual survey on Italy plus occasional specialist surveys.

4.9 Graziani, Augusto. Editor. *L'economia italiana: 1945-1970.* Bologna: Mulino, 1971.
Good introduction to the economy.

4.10 *Journal of Regional Policy.* Naples: Isveimer, 1985-.

A translation of the journal *Mezzogiorno d'Europa,* it provides good coverage of economic conditions (particularly in the South), including a discussion of the budget and the annual report of the Governor of the Bank of Italy.

4.11   *Organisation for Economic Cooperation and Development* (OECD). Paris: OECD, Various Years.
Annual Report on Italy.

4.12   Padoa Schioppa, Fiorella. *Italy. The Sheltered Economy.* Oxford: Clarendon Press, 1993.
One of the best analyses of Italy's economy and economic problems in the 1980s and 1990s.

4.13   Pasinetti, L. Editor. *Italian Economic Papers.* Oxford: Oxford University Press, 1992.
Brings together the best work of Italian economists.

4.14   Podbielski, Gisele. *Italy: Development and Crisis in the Postwar Economy.* Oxford: Clarendon Press, 1974.
Good introduction to Italy's economic development.

4.15   *Review of the Economic Conditions in Italy.* Roma: Banco di Roma, 1979-.
Formerly appeared (1945-1979) with the marginally different title *Review of Economic Conditions in Italy.* Provides useful coverage of current economic conditions.

4.16   Templeman, Donald C. *The Italian Economy.* New York: Praeger, 1981.
A basic introduction to the Italian economy.

ECONOMIC DEVELOPMENT

4.17   Allen, Kevin. MacLennan, M. C. *Regional Problems and Policies in Italy and France.* London: Allen & Unwin, 1970.
A useful comparative analysis of the problems of the South and government attempts to resolve them.

4.18   Bagnasco, Arnaldo. *Tre Italie: la problematica territoriale dello sviluppo italiano.* Bologna: Mulino, 1977.
Path breaking work which identified a differentiated pattern of economic growth in the 1950s and 1960s which, it is argued, created 'three Italies', instead of just the two (North and South) which had previously been assumed to exist. The book helped to generate more than a decade of new research on industrial districts and flexible specialisation both in and beyond Italy.

4.19   Bagnasco, Arnaldo. Triglia, Carlo. Editors. *Società e politica nelle aree di piccola impresa: il caso di Bassano.* Venezia: Marsilio: 1984.
A specialised volume analysing the political and economic functioning of the 'Third Italy' through a case study of Bassano.

4.20   Bagnasco, Arnaldo. Triglia, Carlo. Editors. *Società e politica nelle aree di piccola impresa: il caso di Valdelsa.* Milano: Franco Angeli, 1985.
A specialised volume analysing the political and economic functioning of the 'Third Italy' through a case study of Valdelsa.

4.21   Berger, Suzanne. Piore, Michael J. *Dualism and Discontinuity in Industrial Societies.* Cambridge: Cambridge University Press, 1980.
Contains the best work on dualism in the Italian economy.

4.22   Bianco, I. *Il movimento cooperativo italiano. Storia e ruolo nell'economia nazionale.* Milano: Baldini and Castoldi, 1975.
History of the cooperative movement and its role in national economic development.

4.23   Blim, Michael L. *Made in Italy: Small Scale Industrialization and its Consequences.* New York: Praeger, 1990.
Case study of small firms in the shoe industry in the Marche.

4.24   Bocca, Giorgio. *L'inferno. Profondo sud, male oscuro.* Milano: Arnaldo Mondadori, 1992.
Vivid picture of conditions in the south in the 1990s, portrayed by one of Italy's leading journalists.

4.25   Boccella, Nicola Maria. *Il Mezzogiorno sussidiato: reddito prodotto e trasferimenti alle famiglie nei comuni meridionali.* Milano: Franco Angeli, 1982.
Detailed analysis of family incomes and welfare payments in the South.

4.26   Bonfante, Guido. Et al. *Il movimento cooperativo in Italia. Storia e problemi.* Torino: Einaudi, 1981.
Introduction to the cooperative movement.

4.27   Briganti, Walter. Editor. *Il movimento cooperativo in Italia, 1926-1962. Scritti e documenti.* Roma: Editrice cooperativa, 1978.
First of two volumes of documents and writings on the cooperative movement, this one covering the period 1926-1962. See also [4.28].

4.28   Briganti, Walter. Editor. *Il movimento cooperativo in Italia, 1963-1980. Scritti e documenti.* Roma: Editrice cooperativa, 1981.
Second of two volumes of documents and writings on the cooperative movement, this one covering the period 1963-1980. See also [4.27].

4.29   Castronovo, Valerio. *L'Industria italiana dall'Ottocento a oggi.* Milano: Mondadori, 1980.
Good overview of Italian industrial development.

4.30   Daneo, Camillo. *Breve storia dell'agricoltura italiana 1860-1970.* Milano: Mondadori, 1980.
History of the Italian agricultural sector and its decline after the second world war.

4.31   Donolo, Carlo. Et al. *Classi sociali e politica nel Mezzogiorno: materiali per l'analisi della società meridionale.* Torino: Rosenberg & Sellier, 1978.
Excellent analysis of the social and political structures of the South.

4.32   Earle, John. *The Italian Cooperative Movement: A Portrait of the Lega delle Cooperative e Mutue.* London: Allen & Unwin, 1986.
Introduction to one of the main Italian cooperative associations.

4.33   Giarizzo, Giuseppe. *Mezzogiorno senza meridionalismo. La Sicilia, lo sviluppo, il potere.* Venezia: Marsilio, 1992.
The best example of the new revisionist approach to the Southern Question which attempts to analyse the 'South without meridionalisation'.

4.34   Goodman, Edward. Bamford, Julia. Editors. *Small Firms and Industrial Districts in Italy.* London: Routledge, 1991.
Emphasises the importance and role of the small firm sector and its political environment.

4.35   Graziani, Augusto. Et al. *Lo sviluppo di una economia aperta.* Napoli: Edizioni Scientifiche Italiane, 1969.
Best account in Italian of Italy's rapid economic growth in the 1950s and 1960s, known as the 'economic miracle'.

4.36   Graziani, Augusto. Editor. *Crisi e ristrutturazione dell'economia italiana: diciotto interventi.* Torino: Einaudi, 1975.
Analysis of the crisis of the economy in the 1970s.

4.37   Graziani, Augusto. Pugliese, Enrico. Editors. *Investimenti e disoccupazione nel Mezzogiorno.* Bologna: Mulino, 1979.
Study of investment and unemployment levels in the South.

4.38   Hildebrand, George H. *Growth and Structure in the Economy of Modern Italy.* Cambridge Mass.: Harvard University Press, 1965.
Good early analysis of the economy and its dualistic nature.

4.39   Holmstrom, Mark. *Industrial Democracy in Italy: Workers' Co-ops and the Self-Management Debate.* Aldershot: Avebury, 1989.
Case study of workers' cooperatives in Emilia Romagna.

4.40   Hytten, Eyvind. Marchioni, Marco. *Industrializzazione senza sviluppo. Gela: una storia meridionale.* Milano: Franco Angeli, 1970.
Case study of the effects of introducing big industry into a backward economy: 'industrialisation without development'.

4.41   King, Russell. *Land Reform: the Italian Experience.* London: Butterworth, 1973.
Analysis of the agricultural reforms of the 1950s and beyond.

4.42   King, Russell. *The Industrial Geography of Italy.* London: Croom Helm, 1985.
A basic introduction to Italy's industrial geography.

4.43   Lutz, Vera. *Italy: A Study in Economic Development* Westport: Greenwood Press, 1975.
        Originally published in 1965, the classic account of Italian dualism, although now superseded by work contained in [4.21].

4.44   Mountjoy, Alan B. *The Mezzogiorno*. Oxford: Oxford University Press, 1973.
        A useful introduction to the problems of the South.

4.45   Nanetti, Raffaella. *Growth and Territorial Politics. The Italian Model of Social Capitalism*. London: Pinter, 1988.
        A conceptually innovative model of the Italian political economy based on the dual processes of regionalisation and economic diffusion.

4.46   Onida, Fabrizio. Viesti, Gianfranco. Editors. *The Italian Multinationals*. London: Croom Helm, 1988.
        Analysis of the internationalisation of Italian industry.

4.47   Petriccioni, Sandro. *Politica industriale e Mezzogiorno*. Bari: Laterza, 1976.
        Study of industrial policy and its effects in the South.

4.48   Pezzino, Paolo. *Il paradiso abitato dai diavoli. Società, élites, istituzioni nel Mezzogiorno contemporaneo*. Milano: Franco Angeli, 1992.
        Interesting collection which analyses centre-periphery relations from the broad perspective of the modernisation of the South.

4.49   Piore, Michael J. Sabel, Charles F. Editors. *The Second Industrial Divide: Possibilities for Prosperity*. New York: Basic Books, 1984.
        A general book on flexible specialisation, but one which uses primarily Italian examples.

4.50   Pyke, Frank. Becattini, Giacomo. Sengenberger, Werner. Editors. *Industrial Districts and Inter-Firm Co-operation in Italy*. Geneva: Institute for Labour Studies, 1990.
        Contains detailed studies of flexible specialisation and critical evaluations of its advantages.

4.51   Regini, Marino. Editor. *La sfida della flessibilità*. Milan: Franco Angeli, 1988.
        A collection of the best Italian work on flexible specialisation and the small firm sector.

4.52   Romeo, R. *Breve storia della grande industria in Italia*. Bologna: Cappelli, 1972.
        Basic history of the development of large industry.

4.53   Salvati, Michele. *Il sistema economico italiano: analisi di una crisi*. Bologna: Mulino, 1975.
        Analysis of the crisis of the economy in the 1970s.

4.54   Saraceno, P. *L'Italia verso la piena occupazione*. Milano: Feltrinelli, 1963.
        An example of the optimistic prognoses prompted in the 1960s by Italy's 'economic miracle'.

4.55   Stern, M. R. *Foreign Trade and Economic growth in Italy*. New York: Praeger, 1967.
       Arguably, the best account in English of Italy's export-led 'economic miracle' in the 1950s and 1960s.

4.56   Triglia, Carlo. *Grandi partiti e piccole imprese. Comunisti e democristiani nelle regioni a economia diffusa*. Bologna: Mulino, 1986.
       Based on surveys carried out in the Veneto and in Tuscany, it studies the role played by the ex-sharecropping families in Italy's economic development in the 1950s.

4.57   Triglia, Carlo. *Sviluppo senza autonomia*. Bologna: Mulino, 1992.
       Arguably, the best of the most recent studies of the 'Southern Question', it manages to integrate political, institutional, social and economic factors in such a way as to provide a comprehensive overview.

4.58   Valli, V. *L'economia e la politica economica italiana 1945-1975*. Milano: Etas, 1977.
       Useful analysis of the economy and its dualism and the effects of national economic policy.

4.59   Villari, Rosario. *Il sud nella storia d'Italia: antologia della questione meridionale*. Bari: Laterza, 1974.
       An anthology of key writings on the South over a hundred years.

4.60   Weiss, Linda. *Creating Capitalism: the State and Small Business since 1945*. Oxford: Blackwell, 1988.
       Primarily, but not solely, concerned with Italy, it argues that the small firm sector is linked to the domestic and geopolitical activities of the state.

POLITICAL ECONOMY

4.61   Arrighi, Giovanni. *Semiperipheral Development: The Politics of Southern Europe in the Twentieth Century*. London: Sage, 1985.
       Important comparative volume which locates Italy's political-economic development in relation to its southern and northern neighbours. The comparative framework adopted, and the specific contribution by Peter Lange on Italy, are particularly original.

4.62   Bruni, Franco (ed), *Debito pubblico e politica economica in Italia*. Roma: Sipi, 1987.
       Analysis of the economy and the public debt.

4.63   Cavazutti, F. *Debito pubblico e ricchezza privata*. Bologna: Mulino, 1986.
       Analysis of the budget and public debt.

4.64   Finocchiaro, A. Contessa, A. M. Editors. *La Banca d'Italia e i problemi del governo della monetà*. Roma: Editori Riuniti, 1986.
       Analysis of the Bank of Italy and the problems it faces.

4.65   Galli, Giorgio. Nannei, A. *Il capitalismo assistenziale. Ascesa e declino del sistema economico italiano 1960-1975*. Milano: SugarCo, 1976.
       Argues that Italian capitalism is operated in the interests of the 'state bourgeoisie', politically represented by the DC.

4.66   Giavazzi, Francesco. Spaventa, Luigi. *High Public Debt: the Italian Experience*. Cambridge: Cambridge University Press, 1988.
       Specialist analysis of the Italian experience of public debt, which non-economists might find hard-going.

4.67   Gambale, Sergio. *Struttura e ruolo del bilancio dello Stato in Italia*. Bologna: Mulino, 1980.
       One of the few texts to analyse the workings of the budget in depth.

4.68   Hudson, Ray. Lewis, Jim. Editors. *Uneven Development in Southern Europe: Studies of Accumulation, Class, Migration and the State*. London: Methuen, 1985.
       Useful comparative volume on economic development in southern european countries, including Italy.

4.69   Lange, Peter. Regini, Marino. Editors. *State, Market, and Social Regulation. New Perspectives on Italy*. Cambridge: Cambridge University Press, 1989.
       The best thematic work in English on Italian political economy, adopting an excellent theoretical-comparative framework and analysing the modes of regulation in different policy sectors. Although focused entirely on the Italian case, the book shows how regulation in Italy can be usefully compared with that existing in other countries.

4.70   Monti, Mario. *Il governo dell'economia e della monetà*. Milano: Longanesi, 1992.
       Good overview of economic and monetary policy-making.

4.71   Pedone, Antonio. *Evasori e tartassati: i nodi della politica tributaria italiana*. Bologna: Mulino, 1979.
       Emphasises the difficulties involved in making and implementing economic and financial policies in Italy.

4.72   Puccini, Giusto. *L'autonomia della Banca d'Italia. Profili costituzionali*. Milano: Giuffré, 1978.
       An analysis of the role of the Bank of Italy in relation to economic policy and government.

4.73   Salvati, Michele. *Economia e politica in Italia dal dopoguerra a oggi*. Milano: Garzanti, 1984.
       The best historical analysis of Italian political economy.

4.74   Sapelli, Giulio. *Sul capitalismo italiano. Trasformazione e declino*. Milano: Feltrinelli, 1993.
       Account of the Italian economy which documents the changes of the 1980s and early 1990s.

4.75   Spinelli, Francesco. Tullio, Giuseppe. Editors. *Monetary Policy, Fiscal Policy and Economic Activity: the Italian Experience*. London: Gower, 1983.
Analysis of monetary and fiscal policies.

4.76   Urbani, Giuliano. Editor. *Politica ed economia. Fenomeni politici e analisi economiche*. Milano: Franco Angeli, 1987.
A useful evaluation of the field of political economy and its application to the Italian case.

4.77   Valli, Vittorio. *Politica economica: I modelli, gli strumenti, l'economia italiana*. Roma: La Nuova Italia Scientifica, 1992.
Third edition of a basic guide to the analysis of political economy in Italy.

LABOUR MARKET AND INTEREST GROUPS

4.78   AA.VV (Various Authors). *La politica del padronato italiano*. Bari: De Donato, 1972.
Analyses the political strategy of *Confindustria*, the association of business interests.

4.79   Accornero, Aris. *La parabola del sindacato. Ascesa e declino di una cultura*. Bologna: Mulino, 1992.
The best account available of the development of the trade union movement.

4.80   Baglioni, C. *Il sindacato dell'autonomia: l'evoluzione della CGIL nella pratica e nella cultura*. Bari: De Donato, 1977.
History of the largest trade union, the socialist-communist dominated General Confederation of Italian Workers (CGIL).

4.81   Baldissera, A. *La rivolta dei quarantamila: dai quadri Fiat ai Cobas*. Milano: Franco Angeli, 1988.
Analyses the Fiat strike of the 1980s and its impact on the industrial relations system.

4.82   Barberis, Corrado. *La società italiana: redditi, occupazione, imprese*. Milano: Franco Angeli, 1985.
One of the best analyses of the structure of the labour market.

4.83   Barkan, Joanne. *Visions of Emancipation: the Italian Workers' Movement Since 1945*. New York: Praeger, 1984.
Introduction to the history of the Italian trade union movement.

4.84   Bruni, Michele. De Luca, Loretta. *Unemployment and Labour Market Flexibility*. Bologna: Mulino, 1994.
Excellent study of unemployment and its causes in relation to the structural characteristics of the labour market.

4.85   Cella, Gian Primo. Regini, Marino. *Il conflitto industriale in Italia. Stato della ricerca e ipotesi sulle tendenze*. Bologna: Mulino, 1985.
Provides the best coverage of industrial conflict in Italy.

4.86   Cella, Gian Primo. and Treu, Tiziano. Editors. *Le relazioni industriali*. Bologna: Mulino, 1982.
Provides the best overview of Italian industrial relations.

4.87   *Confindustria*. Bazziche, Oreste (Editor). Vommaro, Riccardo (Editor). *Guida all'archivio storico confindustria: 1910-1990*. Roma: Sipi, 1990.
Useful guide to *Confindustria's* archival contents 1910-1990.

4.88   Contini, Bruno. *Lo sviluppo di un economia parallela: la segmentazione del mercato del lavoro in Italia e la crescita del settore irregolare*. Milano: Edizioni di Comunità, 1979.
Second edition of a work analysing the emergence of the 'black economy'.

4.89   Di Gioia, A. *La scala mobile*. Roma: Editori Riuniti, 1984.
Account of the referendum on the wage indexation system which marked an important turning point in government-trade union relations.

4.90   Ferner, A. Hyman, R. *Industrial Relations in the New Europe*. Oxford: Blackwell, 1992.
This book contains the best work on Italian industrial relations in English in the form of a substantial 76 page chapter by the two editors.

4.91   Ferrarotti, Franco. Editor. *Mercato del lavoro, marginalità sociale e struttura di classe*. Milano: Franco Angeli, 1978.
Analyses the structure of the labour market, focusing on its fragmentation.

4.92   Foa, Vittorio. Editor. *Sindacati e lotte operaie (1943-1973)*. Torino: Loescher, 1975.
Study of trade union and worker militancy, edited by the late trade union leader.

4.93   Fondazione Giovanni Agnelli. *Il sistema imprenditoriale italiano*. Torino: Fondazione Giovanni Agnelli, 1974.
Useful resource on the representation of business interests.

4.94   Gigliobianco, A. Salvati, M. *Il maggio francese e l'autunno caldo italiano: la risposta di due borghesie*. Bologna: Mulino, 1980.
Compares the response of industry and business to the worker militancy in the late 1960s in Italy and France, and in so doing highlights important differences in the relationship between politics and industry in the two countries.

4.95   Golden, Miriam. *Labor Divided: Austerity and Working-Class Politics in Contemporary Italy*. Ithaca: Cornell University Press, 1988.
An analysis of the trade union movement in the 1970s which seeks to explain why some unions adopted a moderate policy while others took a more militant line. Based on considerable amount of primary research.

4.96   Lange, Peter. Ross, George. Vannicelli, Maurizio. *Unions, Change and Crisis: French and Italian Union Strategy and the Political Economy, 1945-1980*. London: Allen & Unwin, 1984.
A comparative study of the postwar strategies of the Italian and French trade union movements.

4.97   Lanzalaco, Lucca. *Lo sviluppo organizzativo delle associazioni imprenditoriali. Il caso della Confindustria* Milano: Franco Angeli, 1992.
One of the best accounts of *Confindustria*, the association for business interests.

4.98   LaPalombara, Joseph. *Interest Groups in Italian Politics.* Princeton: Princeton University Press, 1964.
For a long time, the standard text on Italian interest groups. Even though changes have taken place the basic framework he develops still has relevance today.

4.99   Lungarella, Raffaella. *La scala mobile 1945-1981: caratteristiche, storia, problemi.* Venezia: Marsilio, 1981.
History of the wage indexation system until the end of the 1970s.

4.100   Mattina, Liborio. *Gli industriali e la democrazia: la Confindustria nella formazione dell'Italia repubblicana.* Bologna: Mulino, 1992.
One of the best accounts of *Confindustria*, the association for business interests. Particularly good at disentangling the close relationship between organised business and the Christian Democrats.

4.101   Morlino, Leonardo. *Costruire la democrazia: gruppi e partiti in Italia.* Bologna: Mulino, 1991.
One of the few books which provides an overview of the links between interest groups and political parties. Focuses on the trade unions, *Coldiretti*, *Confagricoltura*, *Confindustria* and their relations with the parties and parliament.

4.102   Paci, Massimo. *Stato, mercato e occupazione.* Bologna: Mulino, 1985.
One of the best analyses of the structure of the labour market.

4.103   Pirzio Ammassari, Gloria. *La politica della Confindustria: strategia economica e prassi contrattuale del padronato italiano.* Napoli: Liguori, 1976.
Good analysis of the strategy of business and industry.

4.104   Pizzorno, Alessandro. *Lotte operaie e sindacato in Italia (1968-1972).* Bologna: Mulino, 1974, 4 vols.
The most comprehensive account of the explosion of worker militancy in the late 1960s.

4.105   Regini, Marino. *I dilemmi del sindacato. Conflitto e partecipazione negli anni settanta e ottanta.* Bologna: Mulino, 1981.
Collection of Regini's articles which together provide a useful overview of the challenges confronting the trade union movement in the 1970s.

4.106   Revelli, Marco. *Lavorare in Fiat da Agnelli a Romiti: operai, sindacati, robot.* Milano: Garzanti, 1989.
Analysis of the changing nature of employer-employee relations inside Fiat, with a good account of the defeat of the 1980 strike which marked a watershed in industrial relations.

4.107   Romagnolo, Umberto. Treu, Tiziano. *I sindacati in Italia: storia di una strategia (1945-1976).* Bologna: Mulino, 1977.
Historical overview of postwar trade union strategy until the mid-1970s.

4.108 Sabel, Charles. *Work and Politics. The Division of Labor in Industry*. Cambridge: Cambridge University Press, 1982.
An important comparative work which attempts to explain how militant industrial action occurs and what its effects are on the industrial and social system. Illuminating insights into the Italian case.

4.109 Tousijn, William. Editor. *Le libere professioni in Italia*. Bologna: Mulino, 1987.
One of the few books available providing an overview of the professions in Italy.

4.110 Trupia, Piero. *La democrazia degli interessi: lobby e decisione collettiva*. Milano: Il Sole 24 Ore libri, 1989.
Analyses the power of the interest group lobby in the political system.

ENTREPRENEURS

4.111 Berta, Giuseppe. *Le idee al potere: Adriano Olivetti tra la fabbrica e la Comunità*. Milano: Edizioni di Comunità, 1980.
Account of the growth of power and success of Adriano Olivetti.

4.112 Comito, V. *La Fiat tra crisi e ristrutturazione*. Roma: Editori Riuniti, 1982.
Good account of the development of Fiat under Agnelli.

4.113 Frankel, P. *Mattei: Oil and Power Politics*. London: Faber & Faber, 1966.
Shows how the controversial character Enrico Mattei built up an industrial empire within the state sector of the economy and how he used this base to build a political network inside the DC.

4.114 Friedman, Alan. *Agnelli and the Network of Italian Power*. London: Harrap, 1988.
A controversial portrayal of Fiat as a network of power which uses unorthodox methods to wield influence and overcome competitors.

4.115 Ronci, D. *Olivetti, anni 50*. Milano: Feltrinelli, 1980.
Account of Olivetti and his typewriter factory in the 1950s which laid the foundations for his long term success.

4.116 Scalfari, Eugenio. Turani, Giuseppe. *Razza padrona. Storia della borghesia di stato*. Milano: Feltrinelli, 1974.
Controversial book by Italian journalists who drew a distinction between the dynamic forces of private enterprise and the sluggishness of the public sector.

4.117 Turani, G. *L'Ingegnere*. Milano: Sperling & Kupfer, 1988.
An account of the success of De Benedetti, the industrialist who became head of Olivetti.

4.118 Votaw, Dow. *The Six-Legged Dog: Mattei and ENI — A Study in Power*. Berkeley: University of California Press, 1964.
An account of the controversial industrialist Mattei who built up an industrial and political power base through his control of state holding companies.

5
Society

GENERAL WORKS

5.1 Ascoli, Ugo. Catanzaro, Raimondo. Editors. *La società italiana degli anni ottantà* Bari: Laterza, 1987.
A useful collection on diverse aspects of Italian society.

5.2 Acquaviva, Sabino S. Santuccio, M. *Social Structure in Italy: Crisis of a System.* London: Macmillan, 1976.
Analysis of Italian society which identifies a structural crisis in the social system. Not an easy, or very rewarding, read.

5.3 Baranski, Zygmunt G. Lumley, Robert. Editors. *Culture and Conflict in Postwar Italy. Essays on Mass and Popular Culture.* London: Macmillan, 1990.
An introduction to major cultural changes of the postwar period.

5.4 Barberis, Corrado. *La società italiana. Esperienze di un secolo.* Milano: Franco Angeli, 1992.
Analyses changes in various facets of Italian society over a period of a hundred years.

5.5 Barlozzini, Guido. Beltramme, Marcello. Editors. *1945-1970. Società, politica, cultura in Italia.* Firenze: G. D'Ama, 1976.
General work on culture and society.

5.6 Barzini, Luigi. *The Italians.* London: Penguin, 1991.
Light introductory reading which both entertains and irritates.

5.7 Bechelloni, Giovanni. Editor. *Il mutamento culturale in Italia (1945-1985).* Napoli: Liguori, 1989.
A most impressive collection analysing a wide range of cultural aspects and processes.

5.8 Caesar, Michael. Hainsworth, Peter R. Editors. *Writers and Society in Contemporary Italy: A Collection of Essays.* London: St. Martin, 1986.
A collection of writings of interest to the beginner and generalist.

5.9   CENSIS (*Centro studi investimenti sociali*). Torino: Fondazione Giovanni Agnelli, Various Years.
Regular surveys and reports on Italian social conditions.

5.10   Eurispes (*Istituto di Studi Politici, Economici e Sociali*). *Rapporto Italia*. Roma: Koinè Edizioni, Various Years.
An annual report of over a thousand pages on society, politics, law and the economy. An indispensable resource.

5.11   Forgacs, David. *Italian Culture in the Industrial Era 1880-1980: Cultural Industries, Politics and the Public*. Manchester: Manchester University Press, 1990.
Links the understanding of cultural production to the process of industrialisation, and in so doing provides a good historical overview of mass cultural changes.

5.12   Forgacs, David. Lumley, Robert. Editors. *Introduction to Italian Cultural Studies*. Oxford: Oxford University Press, 1995.
Good introductory collection to cultural studies in Italy.

5.13   Grasso, Aldo. *Storia della televisione italiana*. Milano: Garzanti, 1992.
Important general history of television.

5.14   Gundle, Stephen. *Italy Transformed: The Communist Party, Cultural Change and Modernization 1943-91*. Cambridge: Cambridge University Press, 1994.
Important book on cultural change and the role played by the Italian Communist Party.

5.15   King, Russell. *Italy*. London: Harper Row, 1987.
Socio-geographic introduction to Italy.

5.16   Haycraft, John. *Italian Labyrinth. Italy in the 1980s*. London: Penguin, 1987.
Beginner's book on Italy, containing good insights and anecdotes.

5.17   ISTAT (*Istituto Centrale di Statistica*). Roma: ISTAT, 1990.
Regular statistical reports and surveys of Italy.

5.18   Lanaro, Silvio. *L'Italia nuova: identità e sviluppo, 1861-1988*. Torino: Einaudi, 1988.
The best history of mass cultural changes since Unification.

5.19   Paci, Massimo. *La struttura sociale italiano: costanti storiche e trasformazioni recenti*. Bologna: Mulino, 1982.
Incisive analysis of the transformation of Italian society in the period until the end of the 1970s.

5.20   Paci, Massimo. *Il mutamento della struttura sociale in Italia*. Bologna: Mulino, 1992.
One of the best analyses of the changes which the Italian social structure has undergone in the 1990s.

5.21   Pasquino, Gianfranco. Editor. *Mass media e sistema politico*. Milano: Franco Angeli, 1984.
       Analysis of the influence of Italian politics on the mass media, in the context of the dominant influence of parties in Italian society.

5.22   Pinto, Diana. *Contemporary Italian Sociology: A Reader*. Cambridge: Cambridge University Press, 1981.
       A sample of the work of Italian sociologists who reject the 'specificity' of the Italian crisis in the 1970s. Some chapters may prove heavy going for the uninitiated.

5.23   Quartermaine, Luisa. Pollard, John. Editors. *Italy Today: Patterns of Life and Politics*. Exeter: University of Exeter Press, 1985.
       A disparate collection, with some good chapters.

5.24   Richards, Charles. *The New Italians*. London: Peguin, 1995.
       Lively and compelling portrait of Italy and the Italians.

5.25   Vertone, Saverio. Editor. *La cultura degli italiani*. Bologna: Mulino, 1994.
       Impressive collection on the culture of the Italians. Attempts to define an Italian 'identity'.

5.26   Ward, William. *Getting it Right in Italy. A Manual for the 1990s*. London: Bloomsbury, 1990.
       Original guide to Italy. Detailed facts and figures on the country as well as outlines of the social, economic and political scene and advice on behavioural norms.

SOCIAL CLASSES AND MOVEMENTS

5.27   Ammassari. Paolo. *Classi e ceti nella società italiana*. Torino: Edizioni Giovanni Agnelli, 1977.
       Contribution to the debate on social classes in the 1970s, sparked off by Paolo Sylos Labini's work [5.39].

5.28   Barberis, Corrado. *La società italiana: classi e caste nello sviluppo economico*. Milano: Franco Angeli, 1976.
       Contribution to the debate on social classes in the 1970s, sparked off by Paolo Sylos Labini's work [5.39].

5.29   Bianchi, Giuseppe. Et al. *I CUB: comitati unitari di base*. Roma: Savelli, 1971.
       Analysis of the joint committees of factory workers and revolutionary groups which grew up in the late 1960s.

5.30   Carboni, Carlo. Editor. *Classi e movimenti in Italia 1970-1985*. Roma: Laterza, 1986.
       Contribution to the debate on the development of social classes.

5.31   Degli Incerti, Davide. Editor. *La sinistra rivoluzionaria in Italia. Documenti e interventi delle tre principali organizzazioni: Avanguardia operaia, Lotta continua, PDUP*. Roma: Savelli, 1976.
Collection of key documents of the three key organisations of the extra-parliamentary left in the late 1960s. Essential resource for researchers.

5.32   Fondazione Luigi Micheletti. *Annali delle Fondazione Luigi Micheletti 1968*. Roma: Fondazione Luigi Micheletti, 1969.
Arguably the best collection on the militancy of 1968.

5.33   Lumley, Robert. *State of Emergency: Cultures of Revolt in Italy from 1968 to 1978*. New York: Verso, 1989.
Explores the cultural continuities between the social movements of the late 1960s and those of the late 1970s.

5.34   Maitan, Livio. *Dinamica delle classi sociali in Italia* Roma: Savelli, 1975.
Important contribution to the debate on social classes in the 1970s.

5.35   Passerini, Luisa. *Autoritratto di gruppo*. Firenze: Giunti Barbèra, 1988.
Provides a vivid description of the extra-parliamentary left in the late 1960s.

5.36   Pizzorno, Alessandro. *I soggetti del pluralismo. Classi, Partiti, Sindacati*. Bologna: Mulino, 1980.
A collection of Pizzorno's most significant writings.

5.37   Rossanda, Rossana. *L'anno degli studenti*. Bari: De Donato, 1968.
Good, if apologetic, account of the student movement of the late 1960s.

5.38   Scalfari, Eugenio. *L'autunno della Repubblica. La mappa del potere in Italia*. Milano: Etas Kompass, 1969.
Overview of the militancy of the late 1960s written at its height by an author who would subsequently become the editor of the influential daily *La Repubblica*. Incisive and critical.

5.39   Sylos Labini, Paolo. *Saggio sulle classi sociali*. Bari: Laterza, 1982.
Originally published in 1974, it sparked off an important debate on social classes in Italy.

5.40   Sylos Labini, Paolo. *Le classi sociali negli anni '80*. Bari: Laterza, 1986.
Sylos Labini's analysis of social classes 'revisited', after the lengthy debate sparked off by his 1974 work [5:39].

5.41   Tarrow, Sidney. *Democracy and Disorder. Social Protest and Politics in Italy, 1965-1975*. Oxford: Clarendon Press, 1989.
A major text which uses the concept of a protest cycle to examine the social movements of the late 1960s. Contrary to the convetional wisdom, the author argues that the terrorist movements of the 1970s did not emerge as a result of the escalation of the activities of the earlier social movements but rather as a product of their decomposition and fragmentation. Roots the analysis in terms of more general questions about the development of Italian democracy.

TERRORISM

5.42   Catanzaro, Raimondo. Editor. *Ideologie, movimenti, terrorismi*. Bologna: Mulino, 1990.
       First of three volumes produced from a research project in the 1980s on left and right wing terrorism in Italy.

5.43   Catanzaro, Raimondo. Editor. *La politica della violenza*. Bologna: Mulino, 1990.
       Second of three volumes produced by a research project in the 1980s on left and right wing terrorism in Italy.

5.44   Catanzaro, Raimondo. Editor. *The Red Brigades and Left-Wing Terrorism in Italy*. London: Pinter, 1991.
       A collection drawn from two Italian volumes [5:42] [5:43], it contains some of the best sociological work in English on Italian terrorism.

5.45   Della Porta, Donatella. Editor. *Terrorismi in Italia*. Bologna: Mulino, 1984.
       Contains some of the best empirical analyses of Italian left wing terrorism available.

5.46   Della Porta, Donatella. *Il terrorismo di sinistra*. Bologna: Mulino, 1990.
       An analysis of left wing terrorism, this is the third volume produced by a research project on left and right wing terrorism in Italy.

5.47   Galli, Giorgio. *Storia del partito armato*. Milano: Rizzoli, 1986.
       Historical overview of Italian left wing terrorism.

5.48   Meade, R. C. *Red Brigades and the Story of Italian Terrorism*. London: Macmillan, 1990.
       Introductory text on terrorism.

5.49   Negri, Antonio. *Proletari e stato*. Milano: Feltrinelli, 1976.
       One of the key works by the professor of philosophy at the University of Padua which helped to inspire left wing terrorism.

5.50   Weinberg, Leonard. Eubank, William Lee. *The Rise and Fall of Italian Terrorism*. Bolder, Co.: Westview Press, 1987.
       A conventional, but useful, study of terrorism, most suitable as an introduction for English readers.

WOMEN AND FEMINISM

5.51   Ascoli, G. Et al. *La questione femminile in Italia dal'900 ad oggi*. Milano: Franco Angeli, 1977.
       History of the women's issue in twentieth-century Italy.

5.52   Baranski, Zygmunt G. Vinall, Shirley W. Editors. *Women and Italy: Essays on Gender, Culture and History*. London: Macmillan, 1991.
       Interdisciplinary collection on women's roles in work and society.

5.53   Bettio, Francesca. *The Sexual Division of Labour. The Italian Case*. Oxford:
        Clarendon Press, 1988.
        Detailed analysis of women's and men's work.

5.54   Birnabaum, Lucia Chiavola. *Liberazione della donna: Feminism in Italy*.
        Middletown CT: Wesleyan University Press, 1986.
        History of Italian feminism in the last thirty years.

5.55   Bono Paola. Kemp, Sandra. Editors. *Italian Feminist Thought: A Reader*. Oxford:
        Blackwell, 1991.
        Key translated writings of Italian feminist thinkers. Includes a bibliography and
        list of women's centres.

5.56   Caldwell, Lesley. *Italian Family Matters: Women, Politics and Legal Reform*.
        London: Macmillan, 1991.
        Charts the legislation passed on women and the family.

5.57   Chianese, Gloria. *Storia sociale della donna in Italia (1800-1980)*. Napoli: Guida,
        1980.
        Social history of women since 1800.

5.58   De Giorgio, Michela. *Le italiane dall'Unità a oggi. Modelli culturali e
        comportamenti sociali*. Bari: Laterza, 1992.
        The first attempt at a comprehensive history of Italian women over the last
        hundred years, but the contemporary period is covered only briefly.

5.59   Hellman, Judith Adler. *Journeys Among Women*. Oxford: Oxford University
        Press, 1987.
        A study of the feminist movement in different cities and regions which emphasises
        the diverse characteristics of the movement.

5.60   Marcuzzo, Maria Cristina. Rossi-Doria, Anna. Editors. *La ricerca delle donne:
        studi femministi in Italia*. Torino: Rosenberg & Sellier, 1987.
        Useful guide to feminist studies in Italy.

5.61   Rossi, Rosa. *Le parole delle donne*. Roma: Editori Riuniti, 1978.
        Analysis of feminist speech and campaigns.

5.62   Weber, M. *Il voto delle donne*. Torino: Biblioteca della Libertà, 1977.
        Analysis of the patterns and significance of women's voting behaviour.

FAMILY AND YOUTH

5.63   AA.VV (Various Authors). *Ritratto di famiglia degli anni '80*. Bari: Laterza,
        1981.
        Sabino Acquaviva and others assess changes in the family in the 1970s.

5.64   Alberoni, Francesco. *Classi e generazioni*. Bologna: Mulino, 1970.
        One of the early works which began the study of youth as a distinctive cultural
        condition.

5.65   Allum, Percy. Diamanti, Ilvo. *'50/'80, vent'anni. Due generazioni di giovanni a confronto*. Roma: Edizioni Lavoro, 1986.
A comparison of two surveys of youth, one in the 1950s and one in the 1980s, which provides a broad picture of socio-economic change in Italy.

5.66   Balbo, Laura. *Stato di famiglia*. Milano: Etas Libri, 1976.
Good overview of the Italian family.

5.67   Banfield, Edward. *The Moral Basis of a Backward Society*. New York: Free Press, 1958.
Propounded the thesis of 'amoral familism' which started a big debate on the South and the peasantry.

5.68   Banfield, Edward. De Masi, Domenico (Editor). *Le basi morali di una società arretrata*. Bologna: Mulino, 1976.
Italian edition of Banfield's famous work [5:67] which also contains a selection of articles from the debate the book generated.

5.69   Barbero Avanzini, Bianca. Lanzetti, Clemente. *Problemi e modelli di vita familiare. Una ricerca in ambito urbano*. Milano: Vita e Pensiero, 1980.
Study of urban family life based on interviews carried out in the 1970s in Milan.

5.70   Barbagli, Marzio. *Sotto lo stesso tetto: mutamenti della famiglia in Italia dal XV al XX secolo*. Bologna: Mulino, 1984.
Impressive analysis of the changes in family structure in the North and Centre.

5.71   Barbagli, Marzio. *Provando e riprovando: matrimonio, famiglia e divorzio in Italia e in altri paesi occidentali*. Bologna: Mulino, 1990.
The only full length text dealing with the impact of legal divorce on the Italian family.

5.72   Bassi, P. Pilati, A. *I giovani e la crisi degli anni settanta*. Roma: Editori Riuniti, 1978.
Study of the impact of the 1970s on youth.

5.73   Cavalli, Alessandro. Cesarea, V. De Lillo, Antonio. Ricolfi, L. Romagnoli, G. *Giovanni oggi. Indagine Iard sulla condizione giovanile in Italia*. Bologna: Mulino, 1984.
The first so-called Iard report on Italian youth, based on wide-ranging interviews in all regions of the country.

5.74   Cavalli, Alessandro. De Lillo, Antonio. *Giovanni anni '80*. Bologna: Mulino, 1988.
The second Iard report on Italian youth, based on wide-ranging interviews in all regions of the country.

5.75   Cavalli, Alessandro. De Lillo, Antonio. Editors. *Giovanni anni '90. Terzo rapporto Iard sulla condizione giovanile in Italia*. Bologna: Mulino, 1995.
The third of the Iard reports on Italian youth, based on wide-ranging interviews in all regions of the country.

5.76   Coletti, A. *Il divorzio in Italia. Storia di una battaglia civile e democratica.*
        Roma: La nuova sinistra, 1974.
        Study of the struggle for divorce legislation.

5.77   Donati, Pierpaolo. *Pubblico e privato, fine di un alternativa?* Bologna: Mulino,
        1978.
        Argues, contrary to Banfield [5:67] that 'familism' has not dominated Italian life.

5.78   Kertzer, David I. Saller, Richard P. Editors. *The Family in Italy. From Antiquity
        to the Present.* New Haven: Yale University Press, 1991.
        An important collection on the family, but (despite the title) largely focused on
        the nineteenth century.

5.79   Melograni, P. Editor. *La famiglia italiana dall'Ottocento a oggi.* Bari: Laterza,
        1988.
        One of the best collections on the transformation of the Italian family.

5.80   Pitkin, Donald S. *The House that Giacomo Built: History of an Italian Family,
        1898-1978.* New York: Cambridge University Press, 1985.
        Excellent anthropological study which shows the effects of industrialisation on
        rural family life.

5.81   Sarti, Roland. *Long Live the Strong: A History of Rural Society in the Appenine
        Mountains.* Massachusetts: Massachusetts Press, 1985.
        Important general study of rural life in the Apennines over the last hundred years.

CHURCH AND RELIGION

5.82   Bucci, Vincent P. *Chiesa e stato: Church-State Relations in Italy within the
        Contemporary Constitutional Framework.* The Hague: Martinus Nijhoff, 1969.
        Study of church-state relations from a legal perspective.

5.83   Burgalassi, Silvano. *Il comportamento religioso degli italiani.* Firenze: Vallechi,
        1967.
        One of the few studies of religious behaviour.

5.84   Candeloro, Giorgio. *Il movimento cattolico in Italia.* Roma: Editori Riuniti, 1982.
        Fourth edition of a general analysis of organised catholicism.

5.85   Chittolini, G. Miccoli, Giovanni. Editors. *Storia d'Italia, Annali, Vol. 9: la
        Chiesa e il potere dal Medioevo all'età contemporanea.* Torino: Einaudi, 1986.
        The ninth volume of Einaudi's history of Italy is focused on the power of the
        church from medieval times until the contemporary period.

5.86   *Dizionario storico del movimento cattolico in Italia 1860-1980.* Torino: Marietti,
        1981-1984. Vol 1: *I fatti e le idee* (1981); Vol. 2: *I protagonisti* (1982); Vol. 3:
        Le figure rappresentative (1984).
        Wide-ranging historical dictionary covering all significant aspects of the Catholic
        movement.

5.87   Evans, Robert H. *Life and Politics in a Venetian Community*. Indiana: University of Notre Dame Press, 1976.
Local case study of a Venetain town which brings out the role of religion in municipal politics.

5.88   Falconi, C. *La chiesa e le organizzazioni cattoliche in Italia (1945-1955)*. Torino: Einaudi, 1956.
Documents the growth of catholic organisations in the immediate postwar period, sponsored by the church.

5.89   Hebblethwaite, Peter. *Pope John XXIII: Shepherd of the Modern World*. London: Doubleday, 1986.
Biography of, arguably, the most significant postwar Pope.

5.90   Jemolo, A. C. *Church and State in Italy*. Oxford: Blackwell, 1960.
Solid, but now dated, account of church-state relations.

5.91   Kertzer, David I. *Comrades and Christians. Religion and Political Struggle in Italy*. Cambridge: Cambridge University Press, 1980.
Anthropological study of Italian working class city life, showing how communist structures, institutions and rituals outplay their religious equivalents.

5.92   Magister, S. *La politica vaticana e l'Italia, 1943-78*. Roma: Editori Riuniti, 1979.
The most comprehensive analysis available of the changes which took place in Vatican policies in the postwar period, particularly under Pope John XXIII and Paul VI.

5.93   Martina, Giacomo. *La chiesa in Italia negli ultimi trent'anni*. Roma: Edizioni Studium, 1977.
General historical overview of the church's role in the first thirty years of the Republic.

5.94   Paulson, Belden. (With Athos Ricci). *The Searchers. Conflict and Communism in an Italian Town*. Chicago: Quadrangle Books, 1966.
Not directly about religion, but an anthropological analysis of a village near Rome which seeks to explain the failure of the church and others to prevent local communist success. Can be usefully compared with work by Kertzer [5.91] and Banfield [5.67].

5.95   Poggi, Gianfranco. *Catholic Action in Italy*. Stanford: Stanford University Press, 1967.
Good study (if now dated) of the largest and most significant of Catholic organisations.

5.96   Pope John Paul II. *Crossing the Threshold of Hope*. New York: Knapf, 1994.
Views of Pope John Paul II on the state of catholicism in the 1990s.

5.97   Prandi, Alfonso. *Chiesa e politica*. Bologna: Mulino, 1968.
Early but useful analysis of the political role of the church.

5.98   Prandi, C. *La religione popolare fra potere e tradizione*. Milano: Franco Angeli, 1983.
Investigation of religious behaviour and an attempt to define and characterise 'popular religion.'

5.99   Riccardi, Andrea. *Il 'partito romano' nel secondo dopoguerra (1945-1954)*. Brescia: Morcelliana, 1983.
Analyses the role of the Vatican in the postwar settlement.

5.100   Riccardi, Andrea. Editor. *Pio XII*. Bari: Laterza, 1984.
Useful collection on Pope Pius XII, who was Pope during the critical reconstruction period (1939-1958).

5.101   Riccardi, Andrea. *Il potere del papa. Da Pio XII a Giovanni Paolo II*. Bari: Laterza, 1993.
An important book documenting the historical power and influence of the Vatican in Italy and beyond.

5.102   Settembrini, D. *La Chiesa nella politica italiana (1944-1963)*. Milano: Rizzoli, 1977.
Studies the role of the Church in politics until the 1960s.

5.103   Yallop, David. *In God's Name. An Investigation into the Murder of Pope John Paul I*. London: Corgi, 1985.
Ultimately unconvincing thesis that Pope John Paul I was murdered, but a worthwhile read for some insights into Vatican politics.

EMIGRATION AND DEMOGRAPHIC CHANGES

5.104   Ascoli, Ugo. *Movimenti migratori in Italia*. Bologna: Mulino, 1979.
Overview of postwar emigration.

5.105   Briani, Vittorio. *Il lavoro italiano all'estero negli ultimi cento anni*. Roma: Italiani nel Mondo, 1970.
Hundred year history of Italian emigrants in search of work.

5.106   Cinel, Dino. *From Italy to San Francisco: The Immigrant Experience*. Stanford: Stanford University Press, 1982.
Analyses the lives of 2,000 Italian migrant families across three generations.

5.107   Cocchi, G. Editor. *Stranieri in Italia*. Bologna: Mulino, 1990.
Good collection on the impact of immigration, a relatively new phenomenon to Italy.

5.108   Cornelisen, Anna. *Flight From Torregreca: Strangers and Pilgrims*. London: Macmillan, 1980.
Humanistic and quite personal study of the lives of those who have emigrated from a village in Basilicata to the North and of those who return.

5.109   Douglass, William A. *Emigration in a South Italian Town*. New Brunswick: Rutgers University Press, 1984.
Detailed case study of emigration from Agnone in Molise.

5.110   Fofi, Goffredo. *L'immigrazione meridionale a Torino*. Milano: Feltrinelli, 1964.
Study of the effects on Turin of the mass immigration from the South in the 1950s.

5.111   Gentileschi, Maria Luisa. Simoncelli, Ricciarda. Editors. *Rientro degli emigrati e territorio*. Napoli: Istituto Grafico Italiano, 1983.
Detailed study of return migration based on four regions: Abruzzo, Friuli-Venezia Giulia, Sardinia and the Veneto.

5.112   King, Russell. Editor. *Return Migration and Regional Economic Problems*. London: Croom Helm, 1986.
Contains three substantial chapters on Italy which analyse return migration in the South (by Russell King, Alan Strachan and Jill Mortimer), in Fruili-Venezia Guilia (by Elena Saraceno), and migrant behaviour in Abruzzo (by Laurence Took).

5.113   King, Russell. *Il Ritorno in Patria: Return Migration to Italy in Historical Perspective*. Durham: University of Durham, Department of Geography, Occasional Publications 23, 1988.
Book-length study of historical phases of emigration and return migration, coupled with a literature review.

5.114   Lopreato, Joseph. *Peasants No More*. San Francisco: Chandler, 1967.
One of the first studies of return migration to the South.

5.115   Reyneri, Emilio. *La catena migratoria*. Bologna: Mulino, 1979.
Case study of the economic effects of emigration from central Sicily.

5.116   Rosoli, Gianfausto. Editor. *Un secolo di emigrazione italiana 1876-1976*. Roma: Centro Studi Emigrazione, 1978.
The most comprehensive history of emigration. Rich in statistical data and graphs.

5.117   Saraceno, Elena. *Emigrazione e rientri: il Friuli-Venezia Giulia nel secondo dopoguerra*. Udine: Il Campo, 1981.
Study of emigration and return migration to a region in the North-East, Fruili-Venezia Giulia. In contrast with the South, return migration has been beneficial to development.

5.118   Sergi, N. Carchedi, F. Editors. *L'immigrazione straniera in Italia. Il tempo dell'integrazione*. Roma: Lavoro, 1992.
Study of immigration into Italy and the urban problems it creates.

5.119   Signorelli, Amalia. Tirritico, Maria-Clara. Rossi, Sara. *Scelte senza potere: il ritorno degli emigrati nelle zone di esodo*. Roma: Officina, 1977.
General study of the social effects of return migration, with an emphasis on housing.

5.120   Thompson, Stephanie Lindsay. *Australia Through Italian Eyes: A Study of Settlers Returning from Australia to Italy*. Melbourne: Oxford University Press, 1980.
Study of the effects of return migration from Australia to the provinces of Treviso and L'Aquila.

MAFIA AND THE UNDERWORLD

5.121   Anselmi, Tina. *Relazione della commissione parlamentare d'inchiesta sulla loggia massonica P2*. Roma: Camera dei Deputati e Senato della Repubblica, Doc. XXIII, no.2, 12 July 1984.
Revealing parliamentary report on the secret masonic lodge P2.

5.122   Arlacchi, Pino. *Mafia Business: The Mafia Ethic and the Spirit of Capitalism*. New York: Verso, 1987.
One of the best accounts of the Mafia in the contemporary period.

5.123   Arlacchi, Pino. *Gli uomini del disonore: la mafia siciliana nella vita del grande pentito Antonio Calderone*. Milano: Mondadori, 1992.
Intriguing conversation with the *pentito* ('supergrass') Antonio Calderone.

5.124   Blok, Anton. *The Mafia of a Sicilian Village 1860-1960: A Study of Violent Peasant Entrepreneurs*. London: Polity, 1988.
Originally published in 1975 by Harper & Row. The fact that Polity has republished it and that the first Italian translation appeared in 1986 is indicative of the continued importance of this historical analysis of Mafia power in a Sicilian village.

5.125   Catanzaro, Raimondo. *Crime as an Enterprise: A Social History of the Sicilian Mafia*. New York: Free Press, 1992.
One of the best accounts in English of the Mafia, with particular emphasis on its contemporary transformation into a system of capitalist enterprises.

5.126   Cecchi, Alberto. *Storia della P2*. Roma: Editori Riuniti, 1985.
History of the secret masonic lodge, P2.

5.127   Cipriani, Antonio. Cipriani, Gianni. *Storia dell'eversione atlantica in Italia*. Roma: Edizioni Associate, 1991.
History of American intervention in Italy and of the 'stay-behind-force', *Gladio*, set up by NATO after the war.

5.128   Cipriani, Gianni. *I mandanti. Il patto strategico tra massoneria, mafia e poteri politici*. Roma: Editori Riuniti, 1994.
The 'secret history' of the Republic from the days of Aldo Moro until the scandal of *Tangentopoli*.

5.129   Cornwell, Rupert. *God's Banker. An Account of the Life and Death of Roberto Calvi*. London: Gollancz, 1983.
An exploration of Italy's corrupt financial underworld through an account of the life and death of one of the principal individuals involved, Roberto Calvi.

5.130 Di Fonzo, Luigi. *St. Peter's Banker: Michele Sindona*. New York: Franklin Watts, 1983.
An exploration of Italy's corrupt financial underworld through an account of the life and death of one of the principal individuals involved, Michele Sindona.

5.131 Falcone, Giovanni. Padovani, Marcelle. *Cose di Cosa Nostra*. Milano: Rizzoli, 1991.
Revealing insights and comments from the leading anti-Mafia crusader of the early 1990s, Giovanni Falcone, who was murdered by the Mafia in broad daylight in 1992.

5.132 Findaca, G. Costantino, S. Editors. *La Mafia. Le Mafie*. Bari: Laterza, 1994.
An excellent collection which brings together nearly all of the contemporary Mafia specialists who analyse the phenomenon from a variety of perspectives. Essential text.

5.133 Galli, Giorgio. *L'Italia sotterranea: Storia, politica e scandali*. Bari: Laterza, 1983.
Overview of the so-called 'secret history' of the Republic.

5.134 Gambetta, Diego. *The Sicilian Mafia: The Business of Private Protection*. Harvard: Harvard University Press, 1994.
Significant contribution to the study of the Mafia. Shows how the Mafia can be studied using the same methodology as for any other industry or business, since the Mafia can be viewed as selling protection.

5.135 Gatti, Claudio. *Rimanga tra noi. L'America, l'Italia, la "questione comunista": i segreti di 50 anni di storia*. Milano: Leonardo Editore, 1990.
The best book available on the so-called 'secret history' of the Republic. Based on a large amount of documents obtained in the United States it analyses the involvement of, amongst others, the CIA and the Italian security services in postwar Italian politics.

5.136 Hess, Henner. *Mafia*. Bari: Laterza, 1973.
History of the Mafia until the 1960s. Although now superseded by more up to date histories, Hess's book is still an indispensable resource for the early pre-war period.

5.137 Lupo, Salvatore. *Storia della Mafia dalle origini ai giorni nostri*. Roma: Donzelli, 1993.
The most complete history of the Mafia from its origins until the contemporary period.

5.138 Mola, Aldo. *Storia della massoneria italiana dalle origini ai nostri giorni*. Milano: Bompiani, 1993.
Comprehensive history of masonry in Italy from its origins until the contemporary period.

5.139 Ramat, Marco. Et al., *La resistibile ascesa della P2*. Bari: De Donato, 1983.
Good collection on the secret masonic lodge, P2.

5.140   Raw, Charles. *The Moneychangers*. New York: Harvill, 1993.
        Journalistic account of the corrupt financial underworld, which lacks the more
        detailed insights which an Italian specialist could have made on the events
        documented.

5.141   Sabetti, Filippo. *Political Authority in a Sicilian Village* Brunswick, NJ: Rutgers,
        1984.
        A case study which shows how the Mafia's mechanisms operate at the village
        level.

5.142   Schneider, Peter. Schneider, Jane. *Culture and Political Economy in Western
        Sicily*. New York: Academic Press, 1976.
        Essential text on the socio-economic conditions in which the Mafia flourishes.

5.143   Shawcroft, Tim. Young, Martin. *On his Honour. The Confessions of Thomas
        Buscetta*. London: Collins, 1987.
        The confessions of the most significant Mafia *pentito* ('supergrass'), Thomas
        Buscetta.

5.144   Tranfaglia, Nicola. *Mafia, politica e affari, 1943-1991*. Bari: Laterza, 1991.
        Useful anthology of documents on the Mafia in the postwar period, with a good
        introduction by Tranfaglia.

5.145   Stille, Alexander. *Excellent Cadavers: the Mafia and the Death of the First Italian
        Republic*. London: Cape, 1995.
        An account of the Mafia in the years 1991 to 1994 and its changing strategies to
        preserve its power base.

5.146   Walston, James. *The Mafia and Clientelism. Roads to Rome in Post War
        Calabria*. London: Routledge, 1988.
        Analyses the role of the Mafia in two local governments in Calabria.

5.147   Willan, Philip. *Puppet Masters. The Political Use of Terrorism in Italy*. London:
        Constable, 1991.
        An account of the manipulation of left wing terrorism by the Italian security
        services and the American CIA. The best guide in English to the Italian
        underworld.

Subject Index

Author Index

140   Author Index

About the Author

MARTIN J. BULL is Senior Lecturer in Politics and Contemporary History and Associate Director of the European Studies Research Institute at the University of Salford. He is coeditor of the book *West European Communist Parties after the Revolutions of 1989* (1994) and is currently working on a book on Italian politics.